Shakespeare: Life, Language and Linguistics, Textual Studies, and the Canon

An Annotated Bibliography of Shakespeare Studies
1623–2000

PEGASUS SHAKESPEARE BIBLIOGRAPHIES

General Editor
RICHARD L. NOCHIMSON
Yeshiva University

Shakespeare: Life, Language and Linguistics, Textual Studies, and the Canon

An Annotated Bibliography of Shakespeare Studies
1623–2000

Edited by
MICHAEL WARREN

Pegasus Press
FAIRVIEW, NC
2002

© Copyright 2002
Pegasus Press
101 BOOTER ROAD
FAIRVIEW, NC 28730

www.pegpress.org

Library of Congress Cataloguing-in-Publication Data

Shakespeare : life, language, and linguistics, textual studies, and the canon : an annotated bibliography of Shakespeare studies, 1623–2000 / Michael Warren, editor.
    p. cm. — (Pegasus Shakespeare bibliographies)
Includes indexes.
    ISBN 1-889818-34-8
    1. Shakespeare, William, 1564-1616 — Bibliography. 2. Shakespeare, William, 1564-1616: — Language — Bibliography. 3. Shakespeare, William, 1564-1616—Authorship—Bibliography. 4. Shakespeare, William, 1564-1616—Criticism, Textual—Bibliography. 5. Shakespeare, William, 1564-1616. Biography—Sources—Bibliography. 6. Dramatists, English—Early modern, 1500-1700—Biography—Bibliography. 7. English language—Early modern, 1500-1700—Bibliography. 8. Canon (Literature)—Bibliography. I. Warren, Michael, 1935- II. Series.
    Z8811.S54 2003
    [PR2894]
    016.8223'3—dc21

2003002367

Cover: Title page of the First Folio. By permission of the Folger Shakespeare Library.

This book has been typeset in Garamond
at Pegasus Press and has been made to last.
It is printed on acid-free paper
to library specifications.

Printed in the United States of America.

CONTENTS

Preface	vii
List of Abbreviations	x
I. Editions of Shakespeare's Plays and Basic Reference Works	
A. Single-Volume Editions of Shakespeare's Plays	1
B. Multi-Volume Editions of Shakespeare's Plays	4
C. Basic Reference Works for Shakespeare Studies	8
II. Life	
A. Documents and Narratives to 1930	18
B. Documents and Narratives since 1930	23
C. Surveys	32
III. Language and Linguistics	
A. General Studies	34
B. Lexicons, Dictionaries, and Concordances; Pronunciation	39
C. Grammar and Rhetoric	46
D. Verse and Prose	54
E. Vocabulary and Imagery	56
IV. Textual Studies	
A. Resources	
1. Bibliography; Bibliographical Surveys	60
2. Facsimiles of Quartos and Folios	61
3. Censuses of Quartos and Folios	63
B. Early Commentary and Editions before 1900	65
C. General Studies	67
D. Quartos Good and Bad	77
E. Revision	83
F. Punctuation	87
G. Editorial Theory and Practice	90
H. Recent Collections of Essays	102

V. Canon
   A. Constitution of the Canon   108
   B. Works Currently Disputed
      1. *Edmund Ironside*   112
      2. *Edward III*   113
      3. *A Funeral Elegy*   114
      4. *The Book of Sir Thomas More*   117

Index I: Authors and Editors (Sections II–V)   121
Index II: Subjects (Sections II–V)   125

PREFACE

The twelve volumes of this series, of which this is the eighth, are designed to provide a guide to secondary materials important for the study of Shakespeare not only for scholars but also for graduate and undergraduate students and college and high school teachers. In nine of the twelve volumes, entries will refer to materials that focus on individual works by Shakespeare; a total of twenty-five plays, plus *The Rape of Lucrece*, will be covered in these volumes. The current volume is one of three that will present materials that treat Shakespeare in more general ways. This is a highly selective bibliography. While making sure to represent different approaches to the study of Shakespeare, the editors are including only work that is of high quality or of great influence or significance.

This volume deals with four extensive, frequently interrelated topics that are fundamental to the study of Shakespeare. Each topic has presented challenges in the selection and arrangement of entries within the section; the aim throughout has been to present readers with convenient access to the most important scholarship upon each topic. Entries for the works included are numbered consecutively throughout the volume. Within each subsection, entries are organized alphabetically by author.

Each entry contains the basic factual information and an annotation. The annotations are designed to be descriptive rather than evaluative; the intention is to convey to the reader the contents of the work being annotated. Readers will find that any evaluative comments appear at the end of an annotation.

The organization of this volume is as follows.

Section I, which will be essentially the same in all twelve volumes, contains those editions and general reference works that in the collective opinion of the editors are most basic to the study of Shakespeare. The annotations in this section have been written by the following series editors: Jean E. Howard, Clifford C. Huffman, John S. Mebane (who has undertaken the updating as well as the composing of the annotations in subsections A and B), Richard L. Nochimson, Hugh M. Richmond, Barbara H. Traister, and John W. Velz.

Section II concerns the Life. The entries in the first two subsections present a record of the construction, interpretation, and reinterpretation of Shakespeare's life and of the documents that constitute the evidence for it; a brief third subsection includes miscellaneous materials that review or survey the writing of lives of Shakespeare. In this section the numerous popular biographies have been ignored. Section III is devoted to Language and Linguistics. The term "Language" is capacious; this section is devoted primarily to studies that deal with the distinctive historical features of Shakespeare's language, its grammar, and its vocabulary. Although some attention is given to distinctive aspects of his usage, no attempt has been made to survey comprehensively the large body of criticism concerned with features loosely described as "style" or "poetry."

The entries in Section IV, "Textual Studies," cover a wide range of topics in a currently burgeoning field of enquiry; this section surveys the early history of the Shakespeare texts, the development and scholarship of the New Bibliography, and the current challenges to conventional critical and editorial traditions. No attempt has been made to include studies of the text of each individual play or poem. For studies of individual texts, the reader should consult the many excellent introductions to major scholarly editions—and, for selected works, the subsections on Textual Studies in the other volumes of the Pegasus Shakespeare Bibliographies series. However, some studies of individual plays are included, where connections are made to broader critical or theoretical issues. In Section V, "Canon," an initial survey of publications relevant to the constitution of the canon of Shakespeare's works is followed by subsections dedicated to four specific texts; these texts were chosen because they seemed to be the most important subjects of current scholarly debate concerning authorship and attribution. Readers should take special care to look for materials concerning these four texts that have been published since the year 2000.

In general, items in this bibliography are not given more than one bibliographical entry. However, five items in Section I are fundamental texts for other sections, and in consequence have been given complementary entries elsewhere. E. K. Chambers, *William Shakespeare: A Study of Facts and Problems*, no. 17, is discussed further in both Section II (as no. 30) and Section IV (as no. 151); S. Schoenbaum, *William Shakespeare: A Compact Documentary Life*, no. 25, is discussed further in Section II (as no. 58); Charlton Hinman, ed., *The Norton Facsimile: The First Folio of Shakespeare*, no. 4, is discussed further in Section IV (as no. 136); David Scott Kastan, ed., *A Companion to Shakespeare*, no. 22, is discussed further in Section IV (as no. 235); and C. T. Onions, *A Shakespeare Glossary*, no. 23, is given an entry (without additional annotation) in Section III (no. 86).

Readers should consult the cross-references at the end of each subsection as well as the subject index (where items are listed by item number only) to see the full range of material relevant to a particular topic. Within the entries, numbers prefaced by "no." indicate cross-references; numbers in parentheses indicate the numbers of the pages in the book or article on which a specific topic is discussed or from which a passage has been quoted.

Abbreviations used are listed on the next page.

Acknowledgements

Michael Warren would like to thank the Committee on Research of the Academic Senate, University of California, Santa Cruz, for its support of this project. He would also like to thank the staff of Reader Services at the Huntington Library and the staff of the McHenry Library at University of California, Santa Cruz, for their assistance.

The editors wish to thank their wives for their support and assistance, and also those colleagues and friends who helped with the compiling of this bibliography.

Michael Warren
University of California, Santa Cruz

Richard L. Nochimson
Yeshiva University

December 2001

Abbreviations

All's Well	*All's Well That Ends Well*
Antony	*Antony and Cleopatra*
Caesar	*Julius Caesar*
chap., chaps.	chapter(s)
Contention	*The First Part of the Contention*
Dream	*A Midsummer Night's Dream*
ed., eds.	edited by/editor(s)
Errors	*The Comedy of Errors*
et al.	and others
F	Folio
Ironside	*Edmund Ironside*
John	*King John*
Kinsmen	*The Two Noble Kinsmen*
Lear	*King Lear*
Love's Labour's	*Love's Labour's Lost*
Measure	*Measure for Measure*
Merchant	*The Merchant of Venice*
Merry Wives	*The Merry Wives of Windsor*
More	*The Book of Sir Thomas More*
MS	manuscript
Much Ado	*Much Ado About Nothing*
no., nos.	number(s)
n.s.	new series
OED	*Oxford English Dictionary*
p., pp.	page(s)
Q	Quarto
repr.	reprint/reprinted
rev.	revised
Romeo	*Romeo and Juliet*
A Shrew	*The Taming of a Shrew*
The Shrew	*The Taming of the Shrew*
Timon	*Timon of Athens*
Titus	*Titus Andronicus*
TLN	through line numbering
trans.	translated by
Troilus	*Troilus and Cressida*
True Tragedy	*The True Tragedy of Richard Duke of York*
Two Gentlemen	*The Two Gentlemen of Verona*
Univ.	University
vol., vols.	volume(s)

I. EDITIONS AND REFERENCE WORKS

A. Single-Volume Editions.

1. Bevington, David, ed. *The Complete Works of Shakespeare.* Updated 4th edition. New York: Addison Wesley Longman, 1997.

Bevington's *Complete Works* includes 38 plays and the nondramatic poems. Introductions, aimed at a broad audience, focus upon questions of interpretation. The general introduction discusses social, intellectual, and theatrical history; Shakespeare's biography and his career as a dramatist; his language and versification; editions and editors of Shakespeare; and the history of Shakespearean criticism. Appendices include discussions of canon, dates, and early texts; brief summaries of sources; and performance history. There are genealogical charts, maps, and a selected bibliography. Emendations of the copy text are recorded only in an appendix; they are not bracketed in the texts of the plays. Spelling is modernized unless an exception is necessary for scansion, to indicate a pun, or for other reasons discussed in the preface. Notes appear at the bottom of the column. Speech prefixes are expanded. Illustrations include photographs from recent performances. Features ranging from the clarity and high quality of the introductions to the readability of the typeface combine to make the texts in this edition admirably accessible to students and general readers. Available with this edition are the BBC's CD-ROM programs on *Macbeth* and *A Midsummer Night's Dream*. These multimedia resources provide the full text and complete audio recordings; footnotes; word and image searches; sources; comments and audio-visual aids on plot, themes, language, performance history, historical background, and characterization; print capability; and clips from film and video performances. A *Teacher's Guide* to the CD provides suggestions for assignments and classroom use.

2. Evans, G. Blakemore, et al., eds. *The Riverside Shakespeare.* 2nd edition. Boston: Houghton Mifflin, 1997.

This edition includes 39 plays, the nondramatic poems, and segments of *Sir Thomas More*. Introductions by Herschel Baker (histories), Frank Kermode (tragedies), Hallett Smith (romances and nondramatic poems), Anne Barton (comedies), and J. J. M. Tobin ("A Funeral Elegy" by W. S.

and *Edward III*) discuss dates, sources, and major interpretive issues. Harry Levin's general introduction discusses Shakespeare's biography, artistic development, and reputation; intellectual backgrounds; Renaissance playhouses and theatrical conventions; Elizabethan English; and stylistic techniques. Heather Dubrow provides an analytical survey of twentieth-century Shakespeare criticism. Evans provides an introduction to textual criticism. Appendices include a history of Shakespearean performance by Charles H. Shattuck and William T. Liston; substantial excerpts from historical documents related to Shakespeare's life and works, including some early responses to the plays; "Annals, 1552–1616," a listing in four parallel columns of events in political history, Shakespeare's biography, theater history, and nondramatic literature; a selected bibliography; indexes; and a glossary. Emendations of the copy text are enclosed in square brackets, and each play is followed by a summary discussion of editorial problems and by textual notes listing the sources of all emendations. Spelling is modernized except for "a selection of Elizabethan spelling forms that reflect ... contemporary pronunciation" (67). Notes appear at the bottom of the column. The volume includes numerous illustrations, including color plates. While the *Riverside* has many features aimed at general readers, the impressive textual apparatus, Evans's fine discussion of textual criticism, and the collection of documents make this edition of special interest to advanced graduate students and to scholars.

3. **Greenblatt, Stephen, Walter Cohen, Jean E. Howard, and Katharine Eisaman Maus,** eds. *The Norton Shakespeare, Based on the Oxford Edition*. New York: Norton, 1997.

This edition includes 38 plays (including quarto, folio, and conflated texts of *King Lear*) and the nondramatic poems, including works of uncertain authorship not included in other single-volume editions. The texts (except for "A Funeral Elegy," ed. Donald Foster) are updated versions of those in the modern-spelling, single-volume *Oxford Shakespeare* (1988) produced by general editors Stanley Wells and Gary Taylor with John Jowett and William Montgomery. The *Oxford* edition is based on revisionary editorial principles, including the belief that some texts previously regarded as having limited authority are in reality records (at times highly imperfect) of early authorial versions later revised in the theater. The revised versions are usually chosen as control texts. In the *Oxford*, passages from earlier versions are often reprinted in appendices; the *Norton* prints these passages from earlier versions, indented, within the texts. *The Norton Shakespeare* provides marginal glosses and numerous explanatory notes; the latter are numbered in the text and appear at the bottom of each page. Textual variants are listed after each work. Stage directions added after the 1623 Folio appear in brackets. Greenblatt's general introduction discusses Renaissance economic, social, religious, and political life; Shakespeare's biography; textual criticism; and aspects of Shakespeare's art, including "The Paradoxes of Identity" in characterization and analysis of the "overpowering exuberance and generosity" (63) of Shakespeare's language. Introductions to individual works discuss a range of historical and aesthetic issues. Appendices include Andrew Gurr's "The Shakespearean Stage"; a collection of documents; a chronicle of events in political and literary history; a bibliography; and a glossary. This edition combines traditional scholarship with a focus on such recent concerns as the status of women and "The English and Otherness." Also available is *The Norton Shakespeare Workshop*, ed. Mark Rose, a set of interactive multimedia programs on CD-ROM that can be purchased either separately or in a package with *The Norton Shakespeare*. The *Workshop* provides searchable texts of *A Midsummer Night's Dream*; *The Merchant of Venice*; *Henry IV, Part Two*; *Othello*; *Hamlet*; *The Tempest*; and Sonnets 55 and 138. Students can find analyses of selected passages, sources, essays that illustrate the play's critical and performance history, clips from classic and from specially commissioned performances, selections of music inspired by the plays, and tools for developing paper topics.

4. Hinman, Charlton, ed. *The Norton Facsimile: The First Folio of Shakespeare.* 2nd edition. Introduction by Peter Blayney. New York: W. W. Norton, 1996.

The First Folio of 1623 is a collection of 36 plays made by Shakespeare's fellow actors, Heminge and Condell. *Pericles, The Two Noble Kinsmen,* and the nondramatic poems are not included. Heminge and Condell claim to have provided "perfect" texts, distinguishing them from what they describe as "stolne, and surreptitious copies, maimed, and deformed by the frauds and stealthes of injurious impostors" (A3). While some of the previously published quartos are regarded today as superior versions, the First Folio indeed provides the most authoritative texts for the majority of Shakespeare's plays. It also includes commendatory poems by four authors, including Ben Jonson, and the Droeshout portrait of Shakespeare. During the two years that the 1623 edition was in press, corrections were made continually, and the uncorrected pages became mingled with corrected ones. In addition, imperfections of various sorts render portions of numerous pages difficult or impossible to read. Hinman has examined the 80 copies of the First Folio in the Folger Shakespeare Library and selected the clearest versions of what appear to be the finally corrected pages. In the left and right margins, he provides for reference his system of "through line numbering," by which he numbers each typographical line throughout the text of a play (the verse and prose of the play as well as all other material such as scene headings and stage directions). In a page from *King John*, for example, which includes what might otherwise be referred to as 3.1.324 through 3.3.74 (this form of reference appears in the bottom margin), the through line numbers run from 1257 to 1380. Appendix A presents some variant states of the Folio text, and Appendix B lists the Folger copies used in compiling this edition. Hinman's introduction discusses the nature and authority of the Folio, the printing and proofreading process, and the procedures followed in editing the facsimile, explaining, among other points, the advantages of through line numbering. Blayney's introduction updates Hinman's discussions of such matters as the status of quarto texts, the types of play-manuscripts available to printers, and the printing and proofreading processes. Blayney also discusses the theory that, since different versions of a given play may represent authorial or collaborative revisions, in such cases there is no "ideal text." No interpretive introductions or glosses are provided. While some valuable facsimiles of quarto versions are available, the Hinman First Folio is clearly an excellent place to begin one's encounter with early printed texts that are not mediated by centuries of editorial tradition.

B. Multi-Volume Editions.

5. Barnet, Sylvan, general ed. *The Signet Classic Shakespeare*. New York: Penguin.

Originally edited in the 1960s, the Signet series was updated in the 1980s; newly revised volumes began to appear in 1998. The 35-volume series includes 38 plays and the nondramatic poems. Collections entitled *Four Great Comedies, Four Great Tragedies*, and *The Sonnets and Nondramatic Poems* are available. Each volume in the newly revised series includes a general introduction with discussions of Shakespeare's biography, including the "anti-Stratfordian" authorship phenomenon; Shakespeare's English; Elizabethan theaters; "Shakespeare's Dramatic Language: Costumes, Gestures and Silences; Prose and Poetry"; editorial principles; and the staging of Shakespeare's plays, including consideration of the concept of the play as a collaboration among the playwright, theatrical ensemble, and audience. Spelling is generally modernized, and speech prefixes are expanded. Explanatory notes appear at the bottom of each page. Appendices contain textual notes, discussion of (and often excerpts from) sources, several critical essays, a survey of each play's performance history, and a bibliography. Although introductions in this series are written for beginning students, the substantial selection of distinguished critical essays is useful for more advanced students, as well.

6. **Bevington, David,** ed. David Scott Kastan, James Hammersmith, and Robert Kean Turner, associate eds. *The Bantam Shakespeare*. New York: Bantam, 1988.

In 1988, 37 plays and the nondramatic poems were published in the 29 volumes of *The Bantam Shakespeare*. Collections entitled *Four Comedies* and *Four Tragedies* are available. Texts, explanatory notes (at the bottom of each page), and interpretive introductions are similar to those of Bevington's *Complete Works of Shakespeare* (see no. 1). Included in the Bantam series are brief performance histories of individual plays and Joseph Papp's forewords on Shakespeare's enduring appeal. Each volume includes a one-page biography of Shakespeare and an introduction to Elizabethan playhouses. Appendices include concise discussions of dates and early texts, textual notes, substantial excerpts from sources, and a brief annotated bibliography. While this series necessarily excludes some of the historical information found in the *Complete Works*, the forewords by an eminent producer/director and the well-written performance histories are engaging features, especially appropriate for students and general readers.

7. **Brockbank, Philip,** founding general ed. Brian Gibbons, general ed. A. R. Braunmuller, associate general ed. *The New Cambridge Shakespeare*. Cambridge: Cambridge Univ. Press, 1982—.

The New Cambridge series will eventually include 39 plays (with *The Reign of Edward III*) and the nondramatic poems. So far, 41 volumes have appeared; among these are two separate editions (one based on an early quarto) of *King Lear*, of *Hamlet*, of *Richard III*, and of *Henry V*. Introductions discuss date, sources, critical history and interpretive issues, staging, and performance history (with numerous illustrations). Discussion of the text precedes each play, and more detailed textual analysis sometimes appears in an appendix. All volumes include a selected bibliography. Spelling is generally modernized; speech prefixes are expanded. Textual notes signaling departures from the copy text and extensive explanatory notes appear at the bottom of each page. Designed for students and scholars, *The New Cambridge Shakespeare* provides more detailed attention to stagecraft and performance history than most other editions. This series succeeds *The New Shakespeare*, edited by Arthur Quiller-Couch and John Dover Wilson.

8. **Knowles, Richard, and Paul Werstine,** general eds. Robert K. Turner,

senior consulting editor. *A New Variorum Edition of Shakespeare.* New York: Modern Language Association.

From 1871 to 1928 H. H. Furness, Sr., and H. H. Furness, Jr., published 19 works of the Variorum Shakespeare. Since 1933, nine new editions have appeared in the MLA series. The completed 40-volume variorum will contain 38 plays and the nondramatic poems. Each volume provides an old-spelling text and a collation of significant emendations from previous editions. Explanatory notes (printed below the textual notes at the bottom of each page) try to record all important previous annotation. Appendices include discussions of a play's text and date. Recent volumes survey the history of criticism and performance and refer to a substantial bibliography; early volumes include excerpts from previous criticism. Sources and analogues are discussed and reprinted. As compilations of scholarship, criticism, and textual analysis, these volumes represent a significant resource for scholars and teachers.

9. Mowat, Barbara A., and Paul Werstine, eds. *The New Folger Library Shakespeare.* New York: Pocket Books, Washington Square Press, 1992—.

Twenty-seven volumes of the New Folger series, which replaces *The Folger Library General Reader's Shakespeare*, appeared between 1992 and 2002. Several new titles will come out each year until the series of 38 plays and the nondramatic poems is complete. Each volume provides a brief initial comment on the play followed by basic introductions to Shakespeare's language and style, his biography, Elizabethan theaters, early editions, and the editorial principles of the series. Half brackets enclose emendations of the copy text; in some volumes square or pointed brackets indicate the sources of passages that appear (for example) only in the folio or an earlier quarto. Explanatory notes appear on pages facing the text, textual notes in an appendix. Spelling is selectively modernized, and speech prefixes are expanded. For each play a different critic offers the "Modern Perspective" that follows the text. A brief annotated bibliography focuses mostly on recent approaches to the play; standard works on language, biography, theatrical setting, and early texts also appear. While this series aims at the broadest possible audience, the clarity and helpfulness of its introductions and explanatory notes make it especially well suited for beginning students.

10. Proudfoot, Richard, Ann Thompson, and David Scott Kastan, general eds. *The Arden Shakespeare.* Walton-on-Thames, U.K.: Thomas Nelson.

The 40-volume *Arden Shakespeare* includes 38 plays and 2 volumes of the nondramatic poems. The edition is continually updated; although some current volumes are from the 1950s, thirteen plays and the Sonnets have appeared in revised third editions in recent years. Introductions provide extensive discussion of dates, texts, editorial principles, sources, and a wide range of interpretive issues. Extensive textual and explanatory notes appear at the bottom of each page. Appendices typically include additional textual analysis, excerpts from sources, and (sometimes) settings for songs. The Arden series often includes scholarship and criticism that are essential for advanced students and scholars. The complete second edition of the Arden series is available on CD-ROM from Primary Source Media. The CD-ROMs enable one to view the edited texts simultaneously with materials from the following: early quarto and folio editions; Bullough's *Narrative and Dramatic Sources* (no. 15); Abbott's *Shakespearian Grammar*; Onions's *Shakespeare Glossary* (no. 23); Partridge's *Shakespeare's Bawdy*; and a 4,600-item bibliography. The complete Arden set is also available on-line, with additional materials for those works that have appeared in the third edition.

11. Spencer, T. J. B., general ed. Stanley Wells, associate ed. *The New Penguin Shakespeare*. London: Penguin Books.

The 40-volume New Penguin series now includes 37 plays and the nondramatic poems; *Cymbeline* is planned. Dates range from the 1960s through 2001. Introductions discuss a range of interpretive issues and are followed by brief bibliographical essays. Explanatory notes follow the text, succeeded by textual analysis, selective textual notes, and (as appropriate) settings for songs. Spelling is modernized, and speech prefixes are expanded. Emendations of the copy text are not bracketed. The New Penguin will appeal especially to those who wish the pages of the text to be free of annotation.

12. Wells, Stanley, general ed. Advisory eds. S. Schoenbaum, G. R. Proudfoot, and F. W. Sternfeld. *The Oxford Shakespeare*. Oxford: Oxford Univ. Press.

Between 1982 and 2002, 27 plays and *Shakespeare: The Complete Sonnets and Poems* were published in the multi-volume *Oxford Shakespeare*. The completed series will include 38 plays and the nondramatic poems. Introductions provide detailed discussion of dates, sources, textual criticism, questions of interpretation, and performance history. Textual notes and extensive commentary appear at the bottom of each page. The commentary and introduction are indexed. Spelling is modernized, and speech prefixes are expanded. The Oxford series is based on revisionary editorial principles, including the belief that some texts previously regarded as of little value are in reality records (at times highly imperfect) of early authorial versions later revised in the theater. The revised versions are usually chosen as copy texts, and appendices sometimes include passages from earlier printed versions. Some appendices include musical settings for songs. Partly because of its editorial principles, this series is of special interest to scholars and advanced students.

C. Basic Reference Works for Shakespeare Studies.

13. Beckerman, Bernard. *Shakespeare at the Globe: 1599-1609.* New York: Macmillan, 1962.

This study of the 29 extant plays (including 15 by Shakespeare) produced at the Globe in its first decade yields information about the playhouse and how Shakespeare's company performed in it. The first chapter, on the repertory system, is based on analysis of Henslowe's diary. Subsequent chapters about the stage itself, acting styles, the dramatic form of plays and of scenes within plays, and the staging derive from study of the Globe repertory. Detailed appendices provide statistics on which Beckerman's analysis partly depends. Beckerman concludes that the style in which these plays were presented was neither symbolic nor what modern audiences would call realistic. Rather, he suggests, passion by the actors was presented within a framework of staging and scenic conventions in various styles according to the needs of particular plays.

14. Bentley, G. E. *The Jacobean and Caroline Stage.* 7 vols. Oxford: Clarendon Press, 1941-68.

Bentley designed his survey of British drama to carry on that of Chambers (see no. 16) and cover the years 1616-42. The 11 chapters in vol. 1 provide detailed information about 11 adult and children's acting companies (1-342); vol. 2 surveys information about actors, listed alphabetically (343-629), with relevant documents reprinted and annotated (630-96), with an index (697-748). Vols. 3, 4, 5 are an alphabetical list, by author, with bibliographical material and commentary, of "all plays, masques, shows, and dramatic entertainments which were written or first performed in England between 1616 ... and ... 1642" (3.v), from "M.A." to Richard Zouche, with a final section (5. 1281-1456) on anonymous and untitled plays. Vol. 6 considers theater buildings (private, 3-117; public, 121-252; court, 255-88; and two that were only projected, 291-309). Vol. 7 gathers together, as appendices to vol. 6, "scattered material concerning Lenten performances and Sunday performances" and arranges chronologically "a large number of dramatic and semi-dramatic events" of interest to students of dramatic literature and theater history (6.v); it includes a general index for vols. 1-7 (129-390), which has numerous references (344-45) to Shakespeare and his plays.

15. Bullough, Geoffrey. *Narrative and Dramatic Sources of Shakespeare.* 8 vols. London and New York: Routledge and Kegan Paul and Columbia Univ. Press, 1957-75.

This work is a comprehensive compendium of the texts of Shakespeare's sources for 37 plays and several poems. Bullough includes analogues as well as sources and "possible sources" as well as "probable sources." All texts are in English, old-spelling Elizabethan when extant, and in some other cases in the compiler's translation. Bullough includes a separate introduction for each play. In the early volumes, interpretation is largely left to the reader; introductions in the later volumes include more interpretation and tend to be longer. There have been complaints of occasional errors in transcription. The major caveat, however, about using this learned, thorough, and imaginative work concerns what Bullough could not conceivably print: the passages in his sources that Shakespeare presumably read but either chose to omit or neglected to include.

16. Chambers, E. K. *The Elizabethan Stage.* 4 vols. Oxford: Clarendon Press, 1923. Revised 1945; with corrections 1967.

In vol. 1, Chambers provides detailed information about the court (1-234): the monarchs, their households, the Revels Office, pageantry, the mask, and the court play. In the section entitled "The Control of the Stage" (236-388), he covers the struggles between the city of London and the court and between Humanism and Puritanism, and treats the status of actors and the socio-economic realities of actors' lives. In vol. 2, Chambers focuses on the history of 38 different acting companies (children, adult, and foreign) (1-294), gives details, such as are known, about an alphabetical list of actors (295-350), and treats the playhouses (16 public and 2 private theaters), including discussion of their structure and management (351-557). In vol. 3, Chambers surveys the conditions of staging in the court and theaters (1-154), the printing of plays (157-200), and then offers a bibliographical survey, including brief biographies, of playwrights alphabetically arranged, from William Alabaster through Christopher Yelverton (201-518). In vol. 4, Chambers concludes that bibliography with anonymous work (1-74) and presents 13 appendices that reprint or summarize relevant historical documents. Chambers concludes this work with four indices (to plays, persons, places, and subjects) to the four volumes (409-67). In these four volumes, Chambers presents an encyclopedia of all aspects of English drama during the reigns of Elizabeth I and James I up to the date of Shakespeare's death in 1616. A subsequent and detailed index to this entire work was compiled by Beatrice White, *An Index to "The Elizabethan Stage" and "William Shakespeare" by Sir Edmund Chambers*. Oxford: Oxford Univ. Press, 1934.

17. Chambers, E. K. *William Shakespeare: A Study of Facts and Problems*. 2 vols. Oxford: Clarendon Press, 1930. Repr., 1931.

This work is an encyclopedia of information relating to Shakespeare. The principal topics of the first volume are the dramatist's family origins, his relations to the theater and its professionals, the nature of the texts of his plays—including their preparation for performance and publication, and also questions of authenticity and chronology (relevant tables about the quartos and metrics are in the second volume). The data available (and plausible conjectures) concerning all texts attributed to Shakespeare, including poems and uncertain attributions, are then laid out title by title. The second volume cites the significant Shakespeare records then available, including contemporary allusions, performance data, legends, and even forgeries (the last two items are more fully covered in Schoenbaum's *Shakespeare's Lives*). There are comprehensive indices and a substantial bibliography. While it is sometimes necessary to update this book by correlation with Schoenbaum's *Documentary Life* (see no. 25) and other, more recent, texts, Chambers's scholarship has been supplemented rather than invalidated by more recent research, and his work remains a convenient starting point for pursuit of background data on Shakespeare's life and works.

18. De Grazia, Margreta, and Stanley Wells, eds. *The Cambridge Companion to Shakespeare*. Cambridge: Cambridge Univ. Press, 2001.

Following a preface, a "partial chronology" of Shakespeare's life and a "conjectural" one of his works, the nineteen chapters of this new edition of the *Cambridge Companion* (the others were 1934, 1971, and 1986) provide a "broadly historical or cultural approach" instead of the earlier volumes' "formalist orientation" (xv). Ernst Honigmann writes on Shakespeare's life (chap. 1), Barbara A. Mowat discusses the traditions of editing (chap. 2, an essay supplemented by Michael Dobson's survey of page- or stage-oriented editions, chap. 15), Leonard Barkan reviews what Shakespeare read (chap. 3), and Margreta De Grazia skims over some aspects of language and rhetoric (chap. 4). John Kerrigan is specific in his discussion of the poems (chap. 5), a specificity balanced by the more general essays of Susan Snyder on the possibilities of genre (chap. 6), Valerie Traub on Shakespeare's use of gender and sexuality (chap. 9), and David Scott Kastan on the use of history (chap. 11). Social background—the City, Court, Playhouse, etc.—are the subjects of chapters by John H. Astington and Anne

Barton (chaps. 7, 8), and Ania Loomba goes farther afield in spotlighting "outsiders" in England and Shakespeare (chap. 10). The last chapters group into two divisions: Shakespeare's posthumous presence in the (British) theater of 1660–1900 (Lois Potter, chap. 12) and in that of the 20th century (Peter Holland, chap. 13), in the cinema (Russell Jackson, chap. 14), on stages and pages worldwide (Dennis Kennedy, chap. 16); and, second, the history of Shakespeare criticism (1600–1900 by Hugh Grady, chap. 17; 1900–2000 by R. S. White, chap. 18). The volume concludes with an annotated list of Shakespeare reference books recommended by Dieter Mehl (chap. 19). Each essay except the last appends its own (further) reading list.

This volume does not precisely replace its immediate predecessor (ed. Wells, 1986, repr. 1991), for the latter's "basic materials ... on Shakespeare's life, ... the transmission of the text, and the history of both criticism and production are still [fortunately] available" (xvi). This availability does not prevent the present volume from printing new essays on some of the same topics; and students, teachers, and scholars may well benefit from comparing the generations—for instance Ernst Honigmann with S. Schoenbaum on Shakespeare's biography, Margreta De Grazia with Inga-Stina Ewbank on Shakespeare and language, Russell Jackson with Robert Hapgood on film (and, in the earlier edition, television) versions of Shakespeare, Hugh Grady with Harry Levin on Shakespeare criticism to about 1900, and R. S. White with the three scholars who wrote three separate essays on his topic, 20th-century Shakespeare criticism. The 1986 edition, then, should be consulted in addition to this new entry.

19. Doran, Madeleine. *Endeavors of Art: A Study of Form in Elizabethan Drama.* Madison: Univ. of Wisconsin Press, 1954.

Doran reconstructs the Elizabethan assumptions about many aspects of dramatic form, defined broadly enough to include genre, eloquence and copiousness, character, and "moral aim." A detailed exploration of classical, medieval, and Renaissance backgrounds makes this a study in historical criticism; however, the cultural context laid out is aesthetic, not ideational. Doran examines the problems of form faced by Shakespeare and his contemporaries—problems of genre, of character, of plot construction—in an attempt to explain the success (or, sometimes, lack of success) of the major dramatists in "achieving form adequate to meaning" (23). Doran's unpretentious, readable study is justly famous as the first book on the aesthetics of Renaissance drama to understand the entire context, to perceive the Renaissance assumptions about dramatic art as a fusion of classical and medieval influences.

20. Gurr, Andrew. *Playgoing in Shakespeare's London.* 2nd edition. Cambridge: Cambridge Univ. Press, 1996.

Gurr focuses on the identity, class, and changing tastes of London playgoers from the opening of the Red Lion in 1567 to the closing of the theaters in 1642. He examines the locations, physical features, price scales, and repertories of the various playhouses, distinguishing particularly between "halls" and "amphitheatres" and rejecting the more common labels "private" and "public." Turning from the theaters, Gurr examines the playgoers, asking such questions as whether they ventured to the playhouses primarily to "hear" a text or to "see" a spectacle. In a final chapter, entitled "The evolution of tastes," he discusses assorted playgoing fashions: from the craze for Tarlton's clowning to the taste for pastoral and romance in the last years of Charles I. Two appendices list identifiable playgoers and references to playgoing during the time period.

21. Gurr, Andrew. *The Shakespearean Stage 1574–1642*. 3rd edition. Cambridge: Cambridge Univ. Press, 1992.

Gurr summarizes a vast amount of scholarship concerning the material conditions of Elizabethan, Jacobean, and Caroline theatrical production. Each of his six chapters provides a wealth of detailed information on theatrical life. The first gives an overview of the place of the theater in urban London from the 1570s until 1642, including an examination of the social status of playwrights, the differences and similarities between the repertories at the open-air amphitheaters (public) and at the indoor playhouses (private), and the changing role of court patronage of theater. Chapter 2 describes the typical composition of London theater companies and their regulation by the Crown. It also gives an historical account of the theatrical companies that at various times dominated the London theatrical scene. In his third chapter, Gurr looks at actors, discussing the famous clowns of the Elizabethan era, prominent tragic actors such as Burbage and Alleyn, and the repertory system within which they worked. The fourth chapter summarizes what is known about the playhouses, including information gleaned from the recent excavation of the remains of the Rose Theater, as well as accounts of the Globe Theater, The Fortune, the hall playhouses, and the Banqueting Hall. Chapter 5 discusses staging conventions and the differences between public and private theaters, and among the various particular theaters, in their use of song, music, clowning, and jigging. Also examined are stage properties and costumes. The final chapter analyzes information about audiences: who went to which kinds of playhouse and how they behaved. Gurr argues that women and all social classes were represented in theatrical audiences, with an increasing tendency in the seventeenth century for the private theaters to cater to a wealthier clientele who demanded a more sophisticated repertory with more new plays. This valuable book concludes with an appendix indicating at which playhouses and by which companies various plays were staged.

22. Kastan, David Scott, ed. *A Companion to Shakespeare.* Oxford: Blackwell Publishers, 1999.

This collection of 28 essays, most with notes and references for further reading, aims to locate Shakespeare in relation to the historical matrix in which he wrote his plays and poems. Following the editor's introduction, the volume is framed by two essays dealing with Shakespeare the man. The first, by David Bevington, deals with what is known, factually, about his life; the last, by Michael Bristol, deals with various myths surrounding the figure of Shakespeare. In between, the book is divided into five sections. The first contains six essays, mainly by historians, dealing with Shakespeare's England, the city of London, religious identities of the period, the family and household structures, Shakespeare and political thought, and the political culture of the Tudor-Stuart period. The second section contains five essays, mostly by literary critics, and discusses readers and reading practices in the early modern period. It includes a general essay on literacy, illiteracy, and reading practices, and four essays focusing on reading, respectively, the Bible, the classics, historical writings, and vernacular literature. The third part of the book deals with writing and writing practices and contains five essays by literary scholars on writing plays, on the state of the English language in Shakespeare's day, on technical aspects of Shakespeare's dramatic verse, on the rhetorical culture of the times, and on genre. These essays are followed by a section on playing and performance. It contains five essays, mostly by theater historians, on the economics of playing, on The Chamberlain's-King's Men, on Shakespeare's repertory, on playhouses of the day, and on licensing and censorship. The final section, consisting of five essays by literary critics, deals with aspects of printing and print culture, including Shakespeare's works in print between 1593 and 1640, manuscript playbooks, the craft of printing, the London book trade, and press censorship. Mixing traditional and newer topics and concerns, *A Companion to Shakespeare* is an up-to-date guide to the historical conditions and the literary and theatrical resources enabling Shakespeare's art.

23. Onions, C. T. *A Shakespeare Glossary.* Oxford: Clarendon Press, 1911. 2nd edition revised, 1919. Repr., with corrections, 1946; with enlarged Addenda, 1958. Enlarged and revised by Robert D. Eagleson, 1986; corrected, 1988.

Onions's dictionary of Elizabethan vocabulary as it applies to Shakespeare was an offshoot of his work on the *Oxford English Dictionary.*

Eagleson updates the third edition with new entries, using modern research (now aided by citations from the Riverside edition [see no. 2], keyed by the Spevack *Concordance* [see no. 26]), while conserving much from Onions's adaptation of OED entries to distinguish Shakespearean uses from those of his contemporaries and from modern standard meanings. The glossary covers only expressions that differ from modern usage, as with "cousin" or "noise." It includes some proper names with distinctive associations, such as "Machiavel," and explains unfamiliar stage directions: "sennet" (a trumpet signal). Many allusions are more fully elucidated, as with the origin of "hobby-horse" in morris dances, or the bearing of "wayward" on *Macbeth*'s "weird sisters." This text, which demonstrates the importance of historical awareness of language for accuracy in the close reading of Shakespeare, now has a brief bibliography of relevant texts. It still needs to be supplemented in two areas: information about definite and possible sexual significance of many common and obscure words appears in Gordon Williams's 3-volume *A Dictionary of Sexual Language and Imagery in Shakespearean and Stuart Literature* (1994); often contradictory guidance about the likely pronunciation of Shakespeare's language is provided by Helge Kökeritz's *Shakespeare's Pronunciation* (1953) and by Fausto Cercignani's *Shakespeare's Works and Elizabethan Pronunciation* (1981).

24. Rothwell, Kenneth S., and Annabelle Henkin Melzer. *Shakespeare on Screen: An International Filmography and Videography.* New York: Neal-Schuman, 1990.

This list of film and video versions of Shakespeare seeks to be comprehensive, covering the years 1899–1989, except that it excludes most silent films, referring the reader to Robert Hamilton Ball's *Shakespeare on Silent Film* (1968). It does include "modernizations, spinoffs, musical and dance versions, abridgements, travesties and excerpts" (x). The introduction, by Rothwell, offers an overview of screen versions of Shakespeare (1–17). The body of the work, with over 675 entries (21–316), is organized by play, listed alphabetically, and within each play chronologically. Represented are 37 plays and the *Sonnets. Pericles* and *Timon of Athens* appear only in the BBC versions in "The Shakespeare Plays" series. For *Hamlet* we have 87 entries. Included also are another 74 entries (317–35) for documentaries and other "unclassifiable" films and videos that present Shakespeare in some form, such as John Barton's "Playing Shakespeare" series and James Ivory's film, *Shakespeare Wallah*. The sometimes quite extensive entries include information about and evaluation of the production, and an attempt to provide information about distribution and availability. The work concludes with a useful selected bibliography with brief annotations (337–45), a series of helpful indices (349–98), and a list of the

EDITIONS AND REFERENCE WORKS 15

names and addresses of distributors, dealers, and archives (399–404).

25. Schoenbaum, S. *William Shakespeare: A Compact Documentary Life.* Oxford: Oxford Univ. Press, 1977. Repr., with corrections, 1978.

An abridged version of Schoenbaum's massive documentary study of Shakespeare published by Oxford in 1975, the *Compact Documentary Life* traces all textual evidence about Shakespeare chronologically from his grandfather's generation up to the deaths of Shakespeare's surviving family members. Legends for which there is no specific documentation—such as the deer-poaching incident—are examined for probability on the basis of surviving materials. Where appropriate, Schoenbaum juxtaposes biographical details with specific passages in Shakespeare's works. Amply illustrated and annotated, this work, unlike Schoenbaum's earlier, larger version and his later (1981) *William Shakespeare: Records and Images*, refers to documents but generally does not reprint them.

26. Spevack, Marvin. *The Harvard Concordance to Shakespeare.* Cambridge: Belknap Press of Harvard Univ. Press, 1973.

This text covers the total of 29,066 words (including proper names) used by Shakespeare in his plays and poems, in the modern-spelling text of *The Riverside Shakespeare* (see no. 2). Stage directions appear in another volume. Contexts are omitted for the first 43 words in order of frequency, mostly pronouns, prepositions, conjunctions, auxiliary verbs, and articles. Individual entries distinguish between prose and verse, and between total and relative frequencies. The modern spelling is not enforced with proper names or significant Elizabethan divergencies: "embassador-ambassador." While the cited context of each use is normally the line of text in which it appears, other limits occur when the sense requires further wording. This concordance helps to locate specific passages and also invites subtler research uses, such as study of the recurrence of words in each play: thus the continuity of *Henry VIII* from *Richard III* appears in their shared distinctive use of certain religious terms. Similarly, accumulated references show the divergence or consistency of meaning or associations for particular terms (Shakespeare's references to dogs are unfavorable). In using this text, one must remember that variant spellings or forms of speech may conceal recurrences of words with the same root or meaning (guilt, gilt, guilts, guilty, guiltily, guiltless), while similar spellings of the same word may have contrasting senses (your grace [the Duke] of York, the grace of God, external grace). The provided contexts reveal the complications, but often are too brief to ensure exact interpretation of a word. The magnitude of the effort involved in this concordance indicates the research gain from electronic procedures, which also permit many permutations of its data, as seen in the nine volumes of Spevack's *A Complete and Systematic Concordance to the Works of Shakespeare* (1968–80).

27. Styan, J. L. *Shakespeare's Stagecraft.* Cambridge: Cambridge Univ. Press, 1967. Repr., with corrections, 1971.

Styan's book explores how Shakespeare's plays would have worked, theatrically, on the Elizabethan stage. Beginning with a discussion of the kind of stage for which Shakespeare wrote and of the conventions of performance that obtained on that stage, Styan then devotes the bulk of his attention to Shakespeare's handling of the visual and aural dimensions of performance. He argues that the scripts guide actors in communicating aurally, visually, and kinetically with an audience. Topics considered include gesture, entrances and exits, the use of downstage and upstage playing areas, eavesdropping encounters, the visual orchestration of scenes involving one or several or many characters, the manipulation of rhythm and tempo, and variations among stage voices. The final chapter, "Total Theater," discusses the inseparability of all the elements of Shakespeare's stagecraft in the shaping of a theatrical event aimed at provoking and engaging the audience's fullest response. The book makes a strong case for studying Shakespeare's plays as flexible blueprints for performance that skillfully utilize and transform the stagecraft conventions of the Elizabethan theater.

Note on Bibliographies

In addition to the above works, readers should be aware of the various bibliographies of Shakespeare studies. Among the most valuable are Stanley Wells, *Shakespeare: A Bibliographical Guide*, Oxford: Clarendon Press, 1990; David M. Bergeron and Geraldo U. De Sousa, *Shakespeare: A Study and Research Guide*, 3rd edition, Lawrence: Univ. Press of Kansas, 1995; Larry S. Champion, *The Essential Shakespeare: An Annotated Bibliography of Major Modern Studies*, 2nd edition, New York: Hall, 1993. Thorough bibliographies for each of a gradually increasing number of plays have been appearing since 1980 in the Garland Shakespeare Bibliographies, general editor William L. Godshalk. An important specialized bibliography is John W. Velz, *Shakespeare and the Classical Tradition: A Critical Guide to Commentary, 1660–1960*, Minneapolis: Univ. of Minnesota Press, 1968 (available on-line). In the special area of Shakespearean pedagogy, a useful (although brief) bibliography appears in Peggy O'Brien, "'And Gladly Teach': Books, Articles, and a Bibliography on the Teaching of Shakespeare," *Shakespeare Quarterly* 46 (1995): 165–72. For information on new materials on

EDITIONS AND REFERENCE WORKS

the study of Shakespeare, readers should consult the annual bibliographies published by *Shakespeare Quarterly* (*World Shakespeare Bibliography*, also available on line), *PMLA* (*The MLA International Bibliography*, also available on-line and on CD-ROM), the Modern Humanities Research Association (*Annual Bibliography of English Language and Literature*, available on-line), and the English Association (*The Year's Work in English Studies*). Ph.D. theses on Shakespeare are listed in *Dissertation Abstracts International*, which is also available on-line.

II. LIFE

A. *Documents and Narratives to 1930.*

28. Aubrey, John. "William Shakespeare." In *Aubrey's Brief Lives*, ed. Oliver Lawson Dick, 275–76. 3rd edition. London: Secker and Warburg, 1958.

In his papers Aubrey (1625–97) records various items of information that he collected about Shakespeare without indicating his sources: that he was born in Stratford-upon-Avon; that his father was a butcher, and that in his boyhood he was a butcher also, and that "when he killed a calf he would do it in a high style, and make a speech"; that he arrived in London at about eighteen and was a good actor; that he was the author of the verse on John Combe. He cites Ben Jonson on Shakespeare's knowledge of Latin and Greek but states that he "understood Latin pretty well"; and he records that in his youth Shakespeare had been a schoolmaster in the country.

29. Brooke, C. F. Tucker. *Shakespeare of Stratford: A Handbook for Students*. New Haven: Yale Univ. Press, 1926.

Brooke reprints 70 items—archival documents such as entries in registers and the will, references in poems, mentions on title pages—relevant to the life, following each with one or more succinct explanatory notes, often with references to others' scholarship; he also reprints (with few notes) the "Chief Contemporary Allusions to Shakespeare's Plays." After essays on the printing of the works, their chronological order, "Metrical Development," and the playhouses, the book concludes with an impressionist critical essay entitled "The Personality of Shakespeare."

30. Chambers, E. K. *William Shakespeare: A Study of Facts and Problems*. 2 vols. Oxford: Clarendon Press, 1930.

See no. 17. This encyclopedic book is the completion of the sequence that began with Chambers's earlier *The Medieval Stage* and *The Elizabethan Stage* (no. 16). In the first three chapters of vol. 1 he reviews Shakespeare's origins in Stratford, presenting the known facts and maintaining a skeptical attitude to the anecdotes and legends without being dismissive; he discusses the state of the stage in London at the time when Shakespeare probably moved there, and then surveys the rest of the life in relation to his known activities in the playhouses and to the surviving documents that refer to him. The rest of the first volume is devoted to the works—the practices of publication in general, the composition of the canon, the chronology, and then the specific textual history of each work (see no. 151). In vol. 2 Chambers reprints in a series of appendixes all the relevant extant documents known to him; each is accompanied by a thorough examination of its contents and its significance. These are followed by a record of contemporary allusions to 1640 and of later biographical data ("The Shakespeare Mythos") to 1866. There is a list of recorded performances of plays (both performances of Shakespeare's plays and performances by companies with which he may have been associated) from 1588–1638. He concludes with a history of the name Shakespeare, a record of spurious documents ("Shakespearean Fabrications"), a table of the quartos, and some metrical tables. In both volumes all the chapters and most of the appendixes are preceded by dense bibliographical notes that summarize the prior scholarship. Each volume contains numerous illustrations—portraits, maps, genealogies, and documents. The narrative of Schoenbaum's *Documentary Life* (no. 59) and the new information discovered since 1930 update Chambers's biography, and Schoenbaum's facsimiles supplement Chambers's transcriptions of documents; however, the density of the data that Chambers provides makes his work still a major resource of documentation.

31. Dowden, Edward. *Shakspere: A Critical Study of His Mind and Art.* London: Henry S. King, 1875.

Dowden constructs a life of Shakespeare as a spiritual history. He delineates initially a writer living simultaneously in both the material and practical world and the world of thought and passion. The two worlds are related in the work, and from a selective reading of the plays and poems, with little or no attention to the facts of the life or to its historical and social circumstances, Dowden describes the career of the artist, finding in the changing subjects of his writing the evidence for a narrative of personal development. In a penultimate chapter on "The Humour of Shakspere" he distinguishes four periods in his artistic life: first, "the tentative period, the years of experiments"; second, "the period of the histories" and "the brightest and loveliest comedies"; third, the "tragic period"; and lastly, a period of "serenity." The clarity of the separation into periods is a consequence of his reliance on the tentative chronology of the works that he derived from F. J. Furnivall. Later in a short "primer," *Shakspere* (New York, Cincinnati, Chicago: The American Book Company, 1877), he names the four periods "In the workshop"; "In the world"; "Out of the depths"; "On the heights," creating a set of categories that exercised considerable influence over succeeding generations but are today regarded as simplistic and inaccurate.

32. *Mr. William Shakespeares Comedies, Histories, and Tragedies.* London, 1623.

In his prefatory poem to the First Folio, "To the memory of my beloved, the Author Mr. William Shakespeare: And what he hath left us," Ben Jonson addresses Shakespeare as "Sweet Swan of Avon," thereby associating the author of the plays with the town of Stratford-upon-Avon, and also ascribes to him a limited education in that he had "small Latin, and less Greek." In another prefatory poem, "To the Memory of the deceased Author Master William Shakespeare," L[eonard] Digges also associates the author Shakespeare with the town of Stratford-upon-Avon.

33. Gray, Joseph William. *Shakespeare's Marriage.* London: Chapman and Hall, 1905.

Gray's primary focus is a study of the interpretation of the two documents concerning the marriage, the bond and the entry in the Bishop of Worcester's register granting a marriage licence. After a scrupulous examination of the various interpretations of both previously advanced, and through an exhaustive study of the bonds issued by the consistory court of the diocese of Worcester, he concludes that there is no reason to presume that John Shakespeare did not consent to the marriage, and that there was no deceit involved in seeking the special licence, only haste; he proposes that the name "Annam whateley" that appears in the licence register is an error for Anne Hathaway. He also includes chapters on the date of Shakespeare's departure from Stratford and various "facts and conjectures" concerning the events of Shakespeare's life. He includes a chronicle of incidents relating to the life of Shakespeare from 1552–1670, and an extensive appendix of original documents with notes.

34. Lee, Sir Sidney. *A Life of William Shakespeare.* London: Smith, Elder, 1898. Revised version, 1915.

In the preface Lee describes his work as a "plain and practical narrative" of Shakespeare's "personal history." Lee produces a conventional description of the major events of the life and records the sequence of the literary productions also; he incorporates the traditional legends of the deer-poaching and the horse-holding. He devotes much space to the discussion of the *Sonnets*, vigorously denying any autobiographical content in them. Lee subjected the book to occasional correction until in 1915 he published the revised version, described on its title page as "Rewritten and Enlarged." This amplified work incorporated into it new research, including his own discovery of the wills of Thomas Combe the Elder and two of his nephews; he specifically denies the identification of Hand D of the *More* manuscript as Shakespeare's, and rejects the arguments for the detection of Shakespeare's practice in punctuation in the published texts (see no. 204). Lee's biography was highly regarded in its time, but it was superseded by E. K. Chambers's *William Shakespeare* (nos. 17, 30).

35. Malone, Edmond. *The Plays and Poems of William Shakespeare.* 10 vols. London, 1790.

Through extensive archival research into the life and examination of the earliest printed evidence Malone endeavors to establish an "authentic" Shakespeare. In vol. 1 he reprints Rowe's "Some Account of the Life etc" (no. 38) with extensive footnotes in which he records the commentaries of Theobald and others. In the footnotes he corrects earlier errors, chastens enthusiasms, and fills in details about Shakespeare's associations with Stratford; he denies his authorship of the verses on John Combe, provides details and an illustration of New Place, and gives information about the lives of the daughters and the death of his son (1: 102–54). He then publishes "additional anecdotes" of Shakespeare, rejecting Samuel Johnson's anecdote about horse-holding as improbable (1: 155–70). He reprints relevant entries from the Register Books of the Parish of Stratford-upon-Avon (1: 171–81); the document granting Shakespeare's coat of arms (1: 182–84); and Shakespeare's will (1: 185–91). See De Grazia (no. 210).

36. *Minutes and Accounts of the Corporation of Stratford-upon-Avon and Other Records 1553–1620.* Transcribed by Richard Savage (vols. 1–3) and by Richard Savage with others (vol. 4), with introduction and notes by Edgar I. Fripp. 4 vols. Vol. 1, 1553–66; vol. 2, 1566–77; vol. 3, 1577–86; vol. 4, 1586–92. (Dugdale Society Publications, vols. 1, 3, 5, 10.) Oxford (vol. 1) and London (vols. 2–4): Oxford Univ. Press, 1921, 1924, 1926, 1929.

Savage and Fripp reproduce documents from various archives, many of which refer to John Shakespeare, William Shakespeare, and their relatives and friends. Fripp's introductions are discursive essays largely on Shakespearean topics that are not always germane to the documents.

37. Munro, John, ed. *The Shakspere Allusion Book: A Collection of Allusions to Shakspeare from 1591 to 1700.* 2 vols. London: Chatto and Windus, 1909. 2nd edition, with a preface by Sir Edmund Chambers, London: Oxford Univ. Press, 1932.

A chronologically arranged series of references to Shakespeare between 1591 and 1700, these volumes include allusions to the works; allusions to contemporary events; allusions to him and his works by his contemporaries and his successors; and legends of Shakespeare and his work. To most entries there are notes signed by the originator. The origins of the collection are described in the continuation subjoined to the title: "Originally compiled by C. M. Ingleby, Miss Lucy Toulmin Smith, and by Dr. F. J. Furnivall, with the assistance of the New Shakspere Society: and now re-edited, revised, and re-arranged, with an introduction, by John Munro." Chambers's preface to the 1932 reprint gives references to subsequent articles that record further allusions. He prints 12 allusions that he thinks warrant immediate inclusion; he also adds some corrections of material in the first edition.

38. Rowe, Nicholas. "Some Account of the Life etc. of Mr. William Shakespear." In *The Works of Mr. William Shakespear*, 1: i–xl. 6 vols. London, 1709.

In "Some Account of the Life," the first continuous life of Shakespeare, Rowe records Shakespeare's family origins in Stratford-upon-Avon, referring to his education at a "Free-School" (1: ii). He relates various tales of his life: the deer-stealing episode; Shakespeare's composition of *Merry Wives* in response to a command from Queen Elizabeth; his playing the Ghost in *Hamlet*; his early sponsorship of Ben Jonson; his composition of verses on Mr. John Combe in his retirement in Stratford. Rowe acknowledges his debt for information about the life to Thomas Betterton the actor, who had earlier journeyed to Warwickshire to gather information about Shakespeare.

39. Smart, John Semple. *Shakespeare—Truth and Tradition*. London: Edward Arnold, 1928.

Smart subjects the traditional history of Shakespeare's life to a scrupulous examination. He describes the background of the Shakespeares and the Ardens in Stratford and its vicinity; proposes that John Shakespeare's personal difficulties may have been the result of his Catholicism; reviews skeptically the legends of Shakespeare's youth, rejecting the deer-poaching and horse-holding stories; rejects the Baconian theory by demonstrating how elaborate the conspiracy of silence would have to have been; and justifies Shakespeare's learning as deriving directly from books without the benefit of university education.

40. Wallace, Charles William. "Shakespeare and his London Associates, as Revealed in Recently Discovered Documents." *University of Nebraska Studies* 10 (1910): 261, 2–100 [sic].

Wallace presents three separate studies of documents that he discovered. In the first he discusses and publishes the documents of the Belott-Mountjoy case in which Shakespeare appeared as a witness; one of the documents bears his signature. The other studies deal with lawsuits that did not concern Shakespeare directly but that provide information about the financial stake that sharers such as Shakespeare had in the Globe and Blackfriars playhouses.

See also nos. 64, 65, 145, 210.

B. Documents and Narratives since 1930.

41. Baker, Oliver. *In Shakespeare's Warwickshire and the Unknown Years.* London: Simpkin and Marshall, 1937.

Although Baker is largely concerned with the buildings, the decorative arts, and the public and working life of the Stratford region, he discusses Shakespeare's ancestry, arguing strongly (against Lee, no. 34) for John Shakespeare's literacy. In the concluding chapters he argues for Shakespeare's leaving Stratford with an acting company; he also reports at length his own examination of the will of Alexander Hoghton of Lea, identifying Shakespeare with William Shakeshafte and hypothesizing that Shakespeare went from the Hoghton household to that of Sir Thomas Hesketh, thence to that of Thomas Hesketh of Gray's Inn, in which environment he would have gained his knowledge of the law.

42. Bearman, Robert. *Shakespeare in the Stratford Records.* Stratford-upon-Avon: Alan Sutton (for the Shakespeare Birthplace Trust), 1994.

Bearman discusses the entries in the Stratford parish register, the records of Shakespeare's purchase of property, land, and tithes, the letters of Richard Quiney to him, and the documents concerning the highways bill and the Welcombe enclosure. He provides a history of the documents and, in an appendix, a list of the 31 items housed at the Shakespeare Birthplace Trust in Stratford-upon-Avon.

43. Bentley, Gerald Eades. *Shakespeare: A Biographical Handbook.* New Haven: Yale Univ. Press, 1961.

Bentley presents a study of the life of Shakespeare that focuses sharply on the surviving documents. He eschews a chronological narrative, organizing his material instead in chapters entitled "Shakespeare in Stratford-upon-Avon," "In London," "The Actor," "The Playwright," "Shakespeare and the Printers," etc. Avoiding speculation in areas of uncertainty, he gives precise explanations of the significance of individual records concerning Shakespeare and his immediate family. Bentley provides succinct expositions of the nature of tithes and enclosures, the London tax rolls, the structure of theatrical companies and their playhouses, and the practices of printing houses and publishers; he summarizes the printing history of the works in quarto and folio, discussing also plays attributed to Shakespeare.

44. Brinkworth, E. R. C. *Shakespeare and the Bawdy Court of Stratford.* London and Chichester: Phillimore, 1972.

Brinkworth describes the contents of two Act Books of the Church Court of the parish of Stratford-upon-Avon that cover the years 1590–1616 and 1622–24 and which are preserved in the Kent Archives Office. He explains the operation of the court, reviews its officers during each period, and discusses the range of moral offences with which it dealt—blasphemy, slander, sexual transgression—and illustrates them with examples. He pays particular attention to the charge made against Susanna Hall, Shakespeare's daughter, of not taking communion, and posits that she may have been a "church papist," one who would attend church but not take communion; he draws attention to similar charges against Hamnet and Judith Sadler, the godparents of Shakespeare's twins. Brinkworth also discusses the charge against Thomas Quiney, shortly before his marriage to Judith Shakespeare, that Margaret Wheeler was pregnant by him. The book concludes with a calendar of the entries of the court's proceedings.

45. Chambers, E. K. "William Shakeshafte." In *Shakespearean Gleanings*, 52–56. Oxford: Oxford Univ. Press, 1944.

Chambers develops a brief observation he made in *The Elizabethan Stage* (no. 16, 1: 280) and did not repeat in *William Shakespeare* (no. 30) to suggest that the William Shakeshafte who appears in the will (1581) of Alexander Hoghton of Lea, Lancashire, may be Shakespeare, and that he may have passed from Hoghton's service as a player to similar employment with Sir Thomas Hesketh, and thence to the company of Lord Strange and the London playhouses. See also nos. 48, 51.

46. Eccles, Mark. *Shakespeare in Warwickshire.* Madison: Univ. of Wisconsin Press, 1961.

Eccles presents an exhaustive survey based on extensive archival research of Shakespeare's life and family associations in and around Stratford. He documents the family histories of the Shakespeares, the Ardens, and the Hathaways: he records details of the lives of neighbors, of persons connected with the grammar school, both teachers and pupils, and of associates of his later years. He also reviews the evidence of acting companies that passed through Stratford before 1590.

47. Foster, Donald W. "Reconstructing Shakespeare." *Shakespeare Newsletter* 41 (1991): 16–17, 26–27, 58–59.

Foster uses the recurrence of "rare" or "secondary" vocabulary in Shakespeare's works to illuminate the life and career. In part 1, "The Roles that Shakespeare Performed," he argues that his system of tests identifies the roles that Shakespeare played, which include Adam and Corin (*As You Like It*), Gaunt and Gardener (*Richard II*), King (*All's Well* and *1 Henry IV*), Ghost (*Hamlet*), and Brabantio (*Othello*). In part 2, "The *Sonnets*," he posits various dates for the composition of different groups of poems in the *Sonnets*, ranging from 1598/99 to 1608. In part 3, "New Directions in Textual Analysis and Stage History," he argues for Shakespeare's authorship of the *Funeral Elegy*. In "SHAXICON 1995" (*Shakespeare Newsletter* 45 [1995]: 25, 30, 32), Foster enlarges his list of roles as a result of running tests on a larger database (SHAXICON) and alters some earlier assignments. Diana Price, in "SHAXICON and Shakespeare's Acting Career," (*Shakespeare Newsletter* 46 [1996], 27–28, 46), challenges Foster's ascriptions, citing the paucity of external evidence for Shakespeare's performing on stage after 1603 in the context of the comparatively ample records for others; Foster defends his method of investigation and his conclusions in "Shaxicon and Shakespeare's Acting Career: Reply to Diana Price" (*Shakespeare Newsletter* 46 [1996]: 57–58).

48. Hamer, Douglas. "Was William Shakespeare William Shakeshafte?" *Review of English Studies*, n.s., 21 (1970): 41–48.

Hamer reviews Chambers's discussions (no. 45, and also *Sources for a Biography of Shakespeare* [Oxford: Clarendon Press, 1946]) of the name William Shakeshafte in the will of Alexander Hoghton and argues that Chambers's "mere conjecture" (*Sources*, 46) identifying him as William Shakespeare is erroneous. He rereads the will to suggest that the word "players" refers to musicians and not to actors; he argues that the form of annuity bequest that includes William Shakeshafte suggests that he was a man of middle years, certainly not a youth of seventeen; he notes the presence of many persons named Shakeshafte in the vicinity of Preston at the time, including several named William; and he denies that Sir Thomas Hesketh maintained a company of players. See no. 51.

49. Honan, Park. *Shakespeare: A Life.* Oxford: Oxford Univ. Press, 1998.

Honan presents a long and full life of Shakespeare, designed for the "general public" but with the standards of scholars in mind, re-examining and re-evaluating all the documentary material to which Schoenbaum refers; on occasions he corrects Schoenbaum's reports. Honan treats the early records and the "myths" of the career with judicious care. He provides extensive discussions of the changing political and social contexts of Shakespeare's life and career as well as of the development of the playhouse and literary cultures in which he worked; the book is dense with information. He writes brief critical studies of the individual poems and plays, placing them within the context of the professional career and occasionally linking their subject matter to events in Shakespeare's private life. In an appendix, "A Note on the Shakespeare Biographical Tradition and Sources for his Life," he summarizes briefly and perceptively the history of the biography of Shakespeare.

50. **Honigmann, E. A. J.** "The Second-Best Bed." *New York Review of Books*, 7 November 1991: 27–30.

Honigmann examines Shakespeare's will in the context of the wills of his contemporaries in the theater, and concludes that it "must be one of the most truly original of original wills" (30). He notes the absence of expected references—to Thomas Quiney and William Hart, and, except in interlineations, to John Heminge, Richard Burbage, Henry Condell, and his wife Anne, who, contrary to convention, is not mentioned by name. He argues that the will itself is "a draft, from which a fair copy was to have been made, had there been time" (28), and proposes that after 25 March 1616, Shakespeare was not well enough to sign his name again; that Shakespeare himself "was largely responsible for its wording and structure" (28). He argues further that the treatment of his wife Anne is slighting and ungenerous, not least in his ensuring that his daughter Susanna should be the unchallenged mistress of New Place. Within the essay he argues that the framing of the indenture in the purchase of the Blackfriars Gate-House was designed to prevent his wife from claiming any rights to the property upon his death. See also E. A. J. Honigmann and Susan Brock, *Playhouse Wills 1588–1642* (Manchester: Manchester Univ. Press, 1993).

51. **Honigmann, E. A. J.** *Shakespeare: the "lost years."* Manchester: Manchester Univ. Press, 1985. 2nd edition, 1998.

Prompted by Chambers's study "William Shakeshafte" (no. 45) and statements from Aubrey (no. 28) and Rowe (no. 38) concerning Shakespeare's early education and career, Honigmann explores the evidence that associates him during the "lost years" (the period prior to Greene's reference to him in 1592 in the playhouse milieu) first with a network of Catholic families in Lancashire including the Stanley family, and specifically Lord Strange. He proposes that Shakespeare was the "William

Shakeshafte" who appears in the will of Alexander Hoghton (1581); that he was preferred to the post of assistant master in his household by John Cottom, a member of a neighbor family to the Hoghtons and formerly the schoolmaster at Stratford; and that he subsequently entered the service of Lord Strange, of whose company of players he became a member. Honigmann suggests that Shakespeare was raised as a Catholic and became a protestant around 1582–85, and that he began writing plays as early as 1586 (*Titus*). He argues in detail for connections between some early plays (*Richard III, Love's Labour's, Dream, 2 Henry VI*, and *3 Henry VI*) and Lord Strange and his family, and between *The Phoenix and the Turtle* and Sir John Salusbury and his family. The conclusion contains a synopsis of his reconstruction of the "lost years." Shakespeare's Catholic upbringing had been proposed previously. In "The Preface to the second edition" Honigmann discusses the reception of the first edition and subsequent relevant studies. Richard Wilson adds further links between Stratford and Lancashire in "Shakespeare and the Jesuits" (*Times Literary Supplement*, 19 December 1997: 11–13). In *Shakespeare: A Portrait Restored* (London: Hollis and Carter, 1957), Clara Longworth, Countess de Chambrun, asserts Shakespeare's Catholic upbringing, a position that she advanced as early as 1927 in *Shakespeare: Actor-Poet* (New York and London: D. Appleton and Company), where she proposed that Shakespeare and Anne Hathaway had already been married by a Catholic priest before the special licence was obtained. See also Peter Milward, *Shakespeare's Religious Background* (Bloomington: Indiana Univ. Press, 1973), in which in the context of discussing the religious background to the works, Milward reviews the evidence advanced by Baker (no. 41) and Chambers (no. 45) and finds "tempting" (41) the identification of Shakespeare with "Shakeshafte." He posits that John Shakespeare was a Catholic recusant, noting that two of the three schoolteachers in Stratford during Shakespeare's school years were Catholics, including John Cottom. See no. 48.

52. Honigmann, E. A. J. "'There is a World Elsewhere': William Shakespeare, Businessman." In *Images of Shakespeare*, ed. Werner Habicht, D. J. Palmer, and Roger Pringle, 40–46. Proceedings of the Third Congress of the International Shakespeare Association, 1986. Newark: Univ. of Delaware Press, 1988.

Honigmann brings together evidence of Shakespeare's financial dealings to suggest that the dramatist was a highly successful businessman notable for the severity of his conduct of his affairs. He draws particular attention to the unusual requirement in his will that his executors, his daughter Susanna and her husband John Hall, pay his other daughter 10 percent interest on a delayed bequest; to Greene's "tiger's heart" gibe as a comment on Shakespeare's usurious activities; and to the records of his family's involvement in moneylending. He concludes that Shakespeare became a very rich man.

53. Jones, Jeanne E. "Lewis Hiccox and Shakespeare's Birthplace." *Notes and Queries* 239 (1994): 497–502.

Jones examines an entry in an inventory of 1627 discovered in Worcester County Record Office, which records a lease held by Lewis Hiccox from William Shakespeare of property in Henley Street; Hiccox is known to have kept in the early seventeenth century an inn in what is now called Shakespeare's Birthplace. Jones describes the details of the inn as recorded in the inventory and relates them as far as is possible to the Birthplace as it survives today.

54. Keen, Alan, and Roger Lubbock. *The Annotator: The Pursuit of an Elizabethan Reader of Halle's Chronicle Involving Some Surmises About the Early Life of William Shakespeare.* London: Putnam, 1954.

Keen and Lubbock discuss the sixteenth-century annotations in a copy of Hall's *Chronicles*, suggesting that they are such as Shakespeare might have made when researching material for the history plays, and that they reflect a mind with Catholic sympathies. Suspecting that they are in Shakespeare's hand, and following the work of Chambers (no. 45), Keen and Lubbock trace the family connections of the person whose name is inscribed in the copy, showing that he was related to a network of Lancashire and Midlands families, including the Hoghtons of Lea, who had associations with Lord Strange, with Catholic recusants, and with families in the Stratford area.

55. Macdonald, Màiri. "A New Discovery about Shakespeare's Estate in Old Stratford." *Shakespeare Quarterly* 45 (1994): 87–89.

Macdonald describes a newly discovered document that refers to the 107 acres of land in the open fields of Stratford that Shakespeare bought from William Combe in 1602. This extract from a deed of exchange in the papers of the family of Sir Simon Archer of Tamworth indicates that Shakespeare settled the land in question on his daughter Susanna and her husband John Hall upon their marriage in 1607.

56. Rogers, Joyce. *The Second Best Bed: Shakespeare's Will in a New Light.* Westport, Conn.: Greenwood Press, 1993.

Rogers discusses the details of the will in the context of an extensive study of the nature of wills in the period and of changes in English law subsequent to the Reformation. She concludes that the will reveals Shakespeare's precise attention to the protection of his family in the forms of the specific grants to Susanna and Judith and the relative absence of reference to his wife Anne, for whom, she asserts, the dower provision precluded any need for bequest. She addresses the question of the "second best bed," discussing specifically a tradition in English law from Anglo-Saxon times of "mortuaries," by which after the best good had been bequeathed to the lord, the second best good (the mortuary) was left to the church, traditionally as a payment for neglected tithes. Rogers suggests that the phrase "second best" should not be read negatively but positively, and that in the will it is capable of bearing a range of associations derived from its ecclesiastical origin, specifically relating to reparation or reconciliation. Rogers considers the suggestion of Jane Cox (see no. 62) that the signatures are not of Shakespeare, but argues that in such a circumstance the will would have to have contained a stipulation acknowledging that fact of another's signing.

57. Sams, Eric. *The Real Shakespeare.* New Haven: Yale Univ. Press, 1995.

In discussing Shakespeare's life and career up to 1594, Sams attacks the mainstream tradition of Shakespeare biography as exemplified by Schoenbaum (see nos. 59, 60) and Wells (see no. 66). Confidently giving credence to the many legends and historical anecdotes, making reassessments of the documentary evidence, and arguing vigorously from internal evidence in the works, he asserts that Shakespeare was trained as a butcher; that he had limited knowledge of Latin; that the family was Catholic; that he may have been implicated in deer-stealing; that he probably was a schoolmaster in Lancashire; that he was trained at some time as a law clerk; that he began his career in the London playhouses around 1585; that the sonnets are strongly autobiographical and date from before 1594; that in his works he was a persistent reviser, and that the lost *Ur-Hamlet*, Q1 *Hamlet*, *A Shrew*, *The Troublesome Reign of King John*, *Contention*, and *True Tragedy* are all examples of early states of plays subsequently rewritten; and that he was the author of *Willobie His Avisa* and probably the author of *Fair Em* and *Locrine* also. In later chapters he rejects the theory of memorial reconstruction of the Bad Quartos and dismisses the concept of collaboration or multiple authorship in *Pericles*, for instance. Sams's work has not received general acceptance.

58. Schoenbaum, S. *William Shakespeare: A Compact Documentary Life.* Oxford: Oxford University Press, 1977. Repr., with corrections, 1978.

See no. 25. To the material already presented in *William Shakespeare: A Documentary Life* (no. 59) Schoenbaum adds a discussion of William Shakeshafte in the will of Alexander Hoghton of Lea (rejecting the identification of Shakeshafte as Shakespeare) and of Anne Shakespeare's rights of inheritance.

59. Schoenbaum, S. *William Shakespeare: A Documentary Life.* Oxford: Clarendon Press in association with Scolar Press, 1975.

In this large format book Schoenbaum presents a full and judicious biography of Shakespeare based on a reexamination of all the documents. He discusses archival records, legends and anecdotes, and the social and historical contexts of the life. He reproduces all the relevant major documents in photographic facsimile of high quality (usually of the original size), including manuscripts, maps, playhouse drawings, and prospects, providing full descriptions of each; he frequently reproduces in facsimile passages from later printed books about Shakespeare. Although Schoenbaum claims to offer no interesting new theories, he discusses in detail all the major issues, particularly the questions arising out of the will in relation to the second best bed and the absence of a bequest of books. On the first issue he argues for Anne's "dower right" as widow "to a life interest of one third in her husband's estate, as well as to residence in the family house" (247); on the second he makes clear that play manuscripts would have been the property of the playhouse and that other books would have been included among his "goods." He pays no attention to the Hoghton will and the possible identity of William Shakeshafte. However, he does discuss them in *William Shakespeare: A Compact Documentary Life* (nos. 25, 58).

60. Schoenbaum, S. *William Shakespeare: Records and Images.* London: Scolar Press; New York: Oxford University Press, 1981.

In a large format book Schoenbaum complements his *Documentary Life* (no. 59) by presenting photographic facsimiles with explanatory commentary of materials relating to Shakespeare, most of which were not included in the *Documentary Life*. He reproduces pages from Simon Forman's "Book of Plays"; the relevant documents concerning the Belott-Mountjoy suit, the purchase of the Blackfriars Gate-House and of New Place, and the Welcombe enclosure; "authenticated" and doubtful and spurious signatures; the pages of Hand D in *More*; the Ireland and Collier forgeries; the Shakespeare portraits; and relevant entries in the Stationers' Register.

61. *Shakespeare in the Public Records.* Public Record Office Handbooks no. 5. London: Her Majesty's Stationery Office, 1964.

This handbook identifies and describes documents in the Public Records directly relating to Shakespeare's life and work. Twenty-eight documents are listed in chronological order, each with an explanation of the contents and significance of the item; among them are the records of the purchase of New Place, the Letters Patent by which the Lord Chamberlain's Men became the King's Men, and the will. Some photographic reproductions are included. There is also a discussion of some suspect documents and an appendix of some documents in the Public Records that relate to members of Shakespeare's family. The preface identifies N. E. Evans as the preparer of the book.

62. Thomas, David. *Shakespeare in the Public Records.* London: Her Majesty's Stationery Office, 1985. (Section on the will and signatures by Jane Cox.)

Thomas describes and reproduces a selection of documents relating to Shakespeare's father and to Shakespeare in London and Stratford; entries concern unpaid taxes on property in London, his deposition in the Belott-Mountjoy suit, references to "Shaxberd" in the account of the Master of the Revels and to his purchase of New Place. Jane Cox discusses the will, which she transcribes in full, and the six "authenticated" signatures. She declares that the signatures on the second and third pages of the will are by the same hand (she does not discuss the first, which is damaged), but that the other three signatures are "not the signatures of the same man" (33); although she states that "there is no positive evidence that Shakespeare did not sign his will" (34), she points out that law clerks commonly forged signatures on documents, and that the will signatures are therefore no more likely than any of the others to be authentic examples of his handwriting. In an appendix there is a fuller list of documents relating to Shakespeare and his family in the Public Record Office.

63. Thomas, D. L, and N. E. Evans. "John Shakespeare in the Exchequer." *Shakespeare Quarterly* 35 (1984): 315–18.

Thomas and Evans describe how John Shakespeare was prosecuted on four occasions in the 1570s on charges of usury and of dealing in wool; they identify some of the other persons in these business dealings and explain the relevant laws. They suggest that the sums of money involved indicate that John Shakespeare's business deals were "on a large scale" (317), and they draw attention to the apparent anomaly of his financial difficulties in the later 1570s.

See also nos. 18, 64, 65, 66, 67.

C. Surveys.

64. Schoenbaum, S. *Shakespeare's Lives.* Oxford: Clarendon Press, 1970. 2nd edition, 1991.

In this guide to the history of the research concerning Shakespeare's life, Schoenbaum reviews initially all the documentary records of the life, including portraits, and also the legends and apocryphal tales associated with Shakespeare's name. He next discusses extensively the work of the first biographers in the eighteenth century and then that of subsequent writers about the life, including anti-Stratfordians. In the first edition the survey of twentieth-century writers ends at 1970. In the revised edition he abridges some of his earlier material, including his study of the documentary records, and brings his survey up to 1989; some illustrations are omitted, and new ones introduced. This book is an invaluable resource concerning the history of Shakespearean biography and the authors.

65. Wadsworth, Frank. *The Poacher from Stratford: A Partial Account of the Controversy Over the Authorship of Shakespeare's Plays.* Berkeley and Los Angeles: Univ. of California Press, 1958.

Wadsworth presents a detailed and frequently ironic survey of the history of anti-Stratfordism. He locates the origins of the rejection of Shakespeare as author in the late eighteenth century, and devotes most of his attention to full discussions of the claims made for Bacon's authorship in the nineteenth century and for that of the Earl of Oxford in the twentieth. Elsewhere he describes more briefly the claims made for candidates such as Sir Walter Raleigh, Sir Edward Dyer, Anne Whateley, Christopher Marlowe, and Queen Elizabeth. Wadsworth describes the characteristics of those who seek to deny Shakespeare's authorship of the works as sincere belief that Shakespeare did not deserve his fame, a militant idealism in relation to the concept of "the Poet," a class-consciousness that cannot allow that a man from Stratford who was not educated at a university could write such plays, and a pervasive romanticism.

66. Wells, Stanley. "Shakespeare's Lives: 1991–1994." In *Elizabethan Theater: Essays in Honor of S. Schoenbaum,* ed. R. B. Parker and S. P. Zitner, 15–29. Newark: Univ. of Delaware Press, 1996.

Wells reviews studies in the life published after the second edition of Schoenbaum's *Shakespeare's Lives* (no. 64); he ranges among both the responsibly scholarly and the irresponsibly fanciful. He draws attention to the contributions to knowledge made by the archival work of Bearman (no. 42), Jones (no. 53), and Macdonald (no. 55), and discusses sympathetically "The Second-Best Bed" by E. A. J. Honigmann (no. 50) and Peter

Thomson's *Shakespeare's Professional Career* (Cambridge: Cambridge Univ. Press, 1992).

67. "The Year's Contribution to Shakespeare Studies: Shakespeare's Life and Times." *Shakespeare Survey* 1–53 (1948–2000): various pages.

Each article contains a survey of recent scholarship concerning the life. With vol. 4 the subtitle changed to "Shakespeare's Life, Times, and Stage." The authors are: vol. 1 Clifford Leech; vol. 2 D. J. Gordon; vols. 3–6 Clifford Leech; vol. 7 Harold Jenkins; vol. 8 I. A. Shapiro; vols. 9–13 R. A. Foakes; vols. 14–15 W. Moelwyn Merchant; vol. 16 Norman Sanders; there was no article in vol. 17; vol. 18–20 Stanley Wells; vol. 21 E. A. J. Honigmann; vols. 22–24 Leah Scragg; vols. 25–27 Nigel Alexander; vols. 28–30 N. W. Bawcutt; vols. 31–32 E. D. Pendry; vols. 33–35 Gāmini Salgādo; vols. 36–38 Lois Potter; vols. 39–44 Richard Dutton; vols. 45–47 Martin Wiggins; vols. 48–50 Mark Thornton Burnett; vols. 51–53 Alison Findlay.

III. LANGUAGE AND LINGUISTICS

A. General Studies.

68. Andrews, John F. *William Shakespeare: His World, His Work, His Influence.* 3 vols. New York: Charles Scribner's Sons, 1985.

In vol. 2, "His Work," three articles appear concerning Shakespeare's language. Marvin Spevack discusses "Shakespeare's Language" (343–61); after a general introduction concerning the challenges of the subject because of the rapid development of the language of the time and Shakespeare's inventiveness over 20 years of that time, he presents a series of studies of orthography, punctuation, phonology, vocabulary, morphology, taxonomy, and syntax. Each is a precise survey of its topic, but the sections on vocabulary and morphology are particularly rich. In "Shakespeare's Poetic Techniques" (363–87) George T. Wright discusses Shakespeare's verse habits in plays and poems, providing a succinct summary of his practice in verse forms, the meter of the plays (in which he demonstrates the various basic patterns of the blank verse line and Shakespeare's phrasing within it), syllabic value, phonetic patterns, and the creation of distinctive speech mannerisms in characters. He includes short studies of rhetorical figures, wordplay, and imagery and image clusters. Brian Vickers contributes a succinct article on "Shakespeare's Use of Prose" (389–95). He discusses prose in relation to character, situation, and plot; he examines the variation from verse to prose, the significance of prose to social status, and its use in relation to psychological state, particularly the representation of madness, or to the assumption of disguise. A bibliography of important related writings follows each article.

69. Barber, Charles. *Early Modern English.* London: Andre Deutsch, 1976. Revised edition, Edinburgh: Edinburgh Univ. Press, 1997.

Barber presents a systematic introduction to the English language between 1500 and 1700. The second edition, an expansion, rearrangement, and updating of the first, begins with the variety of forms of English (regional and social variation, formal and informal speech) and contemporary attitudes (national pride, the felt need for the expansion of vocabulary, writings on rhetoric, the dictionaries and grammar books). He then discusses in separate chapters phonology (changes in vowels, location of stress), morphology (including changes in noun, verb, and pronoun forms), and syntax (including noun and verb phrases, the use of modal auxiliaries). Lastly, he deals with vocabulary, first addressing the addition of loan words from Latin, ancient Greek, and current European and non-European languages, and then discussing changes in the meanings of some words between 1500 and the present day. Barber includes many illustrative examples, short and long; he concludes each chapter with recommendations for further reading.

70. **Blake, N. F.** *Shakespeare's Language: An Introduction*. London: Macmillan; New York: St. Martin's Press, 1983. Reissued as *The Language of Shakespeare*. Basingstoke, U.K.: Macmillan, 1989.

After an introduction in which he focuses on a few specific differences between Shakespearean and current usage, Blake discusses Shakespeare's linguistic environment, attending to the amplification of the language through loanwords and wordplay, to the role of rhetoric, and to the experiments with alphabets. His discussion of "Varieties" in dialects, forms of address, oaths, and alternative verb inflections is followed by an examination of early modern variants in vocabulary and the capacity for word formation; Blake emphasizes Shakespeare's distinctive practice of functional shift, using nouns as verbs. Three chapters are devoted to precise studies with numerous illustrations of Shakespeare's particular flexible habits with nominal groups, verbal groups, and with adverbs, prepositions, and conjunctions; he states that the nominal group "is the principal vehicle for his meaning and it encapsulates much of the metaphor and imagery" (80). His consideration of word order and sentence types includes a commentary on the problems of interpreting the punctuation of the quarto and Folio texts. He concludes with an examination of a passage from *Troilus* in the light of his prior demonstration of Shakespeare's distinctive linguistic features. See also N. F. Blake, *Essays on Shakespeare's Language 1st series* (Misterton, U.K.: Language Press, 1996).

71. **Blake, Norman.** "Studies on Shakespeare's Language: An overview." In *The Shakespearean International Yearbook*, ed. W. R. Elton and John M. Mucciolo, 168–86. Aldershot, U.K.: Ashgate, 1999.

Blake provides "a cursory survey of where we stand today in language studies in Shakespeare" (182). He discusses the major texts and the characteristics and directions of the most recent work under the following headings: "Grammars," "Dictionaries and Glossaries," "Punctuation and Orthography," "Phonology," "Syntax," "General Studies," and "Modern Linguistic Approaches." He pays no attention to style or rhetoric. This brief essay provides an excellent introduction to the subject, not least because of the extensive references in the footnotes.

72. Bolton, W. F. *Shakespeare's English.* Oxford: Basil Blackwell, 1992.

Attentive to the problems that derive from the various origins of the texts of Shakespeare's plays, Bolton presents seven illuminating and densely informative studies, each of which focuses on a different topic or set of topics and takes its illustrations from one or more of the ten history plays. The initial studies, in which the advantage gained from the assistance of computer databases is evident, are focused on linguistic data and provide detailed examinations of many passages from the plays: pronunciation, rhyme, and meter in *Richard III*; linguistic structure with particular attention to syntax in *Richard II*; vocabulary in *John*; rhetoric in the *Henry VI* plays. The later studies concern linguistic variety in the *Henry IV* plays, pragmatics in *Henry VIII*, and language and nation in *Henry V*.

73. Brook, G. L. *The Language of Shakespeare.* London: Andre Deutsch, 1976.

Brook provides a comprehensive and detailed study of Shakespeare's language. After an introduction that stresses the variousness of English in Shakespeare's time, Brook devotes chapters to: vocabulary, in which he emphasizes the blend of old and new words, Shakespeare's innovations and coinings, and the differences of meanings of particular words in his language and in modern English; syntax and accidence, in which he presents a detailed study of distinctive features of grammatical usage, including subject-verb agreements, pronoun use (thou/you), and verb forms; Shakespeare's habits in word-formation; pronunciation, spelling, and punctuation, in which he insists on the value of old-spelling texts as the foundation for scholarly observation; meter; rhetoric; and dialects, registers, and idiolects, in which he states that Shakespeare generally uses Southern dialect, rather than that of his native Warwickshire, when he wishes to represent a distinctive dialect, although Brook then gives an analysis of the features of other regional forms that Shakespeare uses for characterization.

74. Hope, Jonathan. "Shakespeare's 'Native English.'" In *A Companion to Shakespeare*, ed. David Scott Kastan, 239–55. Oxford: Blackwell, 1999.

After briefly establishing the changing role and status of English during Shakespeare's lifetime Hope surveys its distinctive features as an unstandarized language. He discusses the range of spellings and options within grammar: the use of "-s" and "-eth" in third person singular verbs, the formation of questions and commands with or without "do," and the discriminations entailed in the choice of "thou" or "you"—power, solidarity, and emotional attitude. With regard to vocabulary he reviews the history of English borrowing from French and Latin and the cultivation of deliberate borrowing in the period; in this context Hope suggests that Shakespeare should be considered as deriving new words by the addition of prefixes and by functional shift rather than coining them. Within phonology he describes the significance of the Great Vowel Shift and notes some instances of difference in stress from current English. He closes by describing Shakespeare as "tend[ing] to lag behind grammatical change" (253), illustrating his point by an examination of the rich variety of language use in *Merry Wives*.

75. Hussey, S. S. *The Literary Language of Shakespeare.* London: Longman, 1982. 2nd edition, 1992.

In both editions Hussey presents a study of Shakespeare's language in the context initially of the history of English and then of his dramatic practice. Although the overall design of the editions is the same, the second is revised throughout, much material is reorganized and amplified, and a new section added (see below). He argues that English writers were very attentive to the condition of English and self-conscious in the development of its resources. In a series of chapters he examines the various strategies they employed: the development of amplitude of expression (*copia*), especially in vocabulary through doublets and compounds, and the introduction of Latinisms; the exploitation of rhetoric in syntax, particularly in prose—especially the Ciceronian and euphuistic styles. He also analyzes grammatical forms characteristic of the period. On this foundation he then discusses Shakespeare's practice in the plays. In "Register and Style," he examines the variety of styles available and how they communicate in drama; he identifies possible idiolects in the plays, examines the construction and exploitation of colloquial language, and then presents a series of studies concerning (among other things) the use of prose, the idea of a "Roman" style, and the development of the soliloquy. In the second edition he concludes with a chapter entitled "Four Plays," in which he presents succinct studies of *Henry V, As You Like It, Macbeth*, and *The Winter's Tale* in terms of the linguistic features he has previously described.

76. Partridge, A. C. *The Language of Renaissance Poetry: Spenser, Shakespeare, Donne, Milton.* London: Andre Deutsch, 1971.

In chapter 1, "Introductory Notes on Method" (11–27), Partridge proposes to attend to five aspects of language: word choice, movement (metrics), grammatical structure, meaning, and rhetorical devices. He devotes three chapters to the study of Shakespeare, demonstrating the changes in his verbal practices. He begins each chapter with general remarks and then proceeds to the systematic and detailed analysis of specimen passages. In chapter 5, "Non-Dramatic Poetry: Marlowe and Shakespeare" (102–40), he considers several *Sonnets* and excerpts from *Venus and Adonis*; in chapter 6, "Shakespeare's Declamatory and Lyrical Dramas (to 1600)" (141–84), he examines speeches from *Richard III*, *Richard II*, *Romeo*, and *Merchant*; in chapter 7, "Shakespeare's Plays after 1600" (185–230), examples from *Hamlet*, *Othello*, *Timon*, *Lear*, *Macbeth*, *Antony*, and *Tempest* demonstrate the shift toward a reconciliation of blank verse with natural speech rhythms.

77. Partridge, A. C. "Shakespeare's English: A bibliographical survey." *Poetica* (Tokyo) 11 (1979): 46–79.

Partridge presents a useful summary of work since 1920 concerning Shakespeare's English. He divides his subject into two groups, each of seven topics: in the category of language are included vocabulary, meaning, accidence, syntax, orthography, punctuation, and pronunciation; stylistics includes rhetoric, poetic style, versification, prose style, wordplay, proverbs, and miscellaneous. Each of the 14 sections begins with a succinct summary and assessment of the major work in the area; topic bibliographies, which have between 10 and 40 entries, are organized into separate lists of books and articles. Individual entries are not annotated.

78. Ronberg, Gert. *A Way With Words: The Language of English Renaissance Literature*. London: Edward Arnold, 1992.

Ronberg devotes two short initial chapters to sounds, variations in stress, and variety in spelling, and to vocabulary and meaning. In chapter 3 he examines syntax, specifically in relation to verbs and pronouns, with a section on "thou/you" (75–88), and in chapter 4 he discusses sentence structures in the period, with a section on punctuation (116–27). Chapter 5 provides a survey of the origin and development of rhetoric in the period, a glossary of rhetorical terms, and rhetorical analyses of several passages. Ronberg aims his book at a student readership; although he draws on a range of authors for his examples, a considerable proportion of the illustrations are from Shakespeare.

79. Salmon, Vivian, and Edwina Burness, eds. *A Reader in the Language of Shakespearean Drama*. Amsterdam Studies in the Theory and History of Linguistic Science, series 3—Studies in the History of the Language Sciences, vol. 35. Amsterdam and Philadelphia: John Benjamins, 1987.

Comprised of 33 previously published articles from various sources, each reproduced in photographic facsimile, and with an introduction by Vivian Salmon, this collection contains essays of three basic types: first, essays that explain differences in language usage of Shakespeare's time and thereby clarify meaning for the modern reader; second, essays that explore Shakespeare's distinctive and creative exploitation of his contemporary linguistic resources; and third, essays that investigate Elizabethan English through the Shakespearean dramatic text. The essays are assembled under the following categories: "Shakespeare and the English Language"; "Aspects of Colloquial Elizabethan English"; "Studies in Vocabulary"; "Shakespeare and Elizabethan Grammar"; "Studies in Rhetoric and Metre"; "Punctuation"; "The Linguistic Context of Shakespearean Drama." Many of the articles are discussed in this bibliography; see nos. 99, 109, 110, 111, 115, 125, 127.

See also nos. 109, 244.

B. Lexicons, Dictionaries, and Concordances; Pronunciation.

80. Cercignani, Fausto. *Shakespeare's Words and Elizabethan Pronunciation.* Oxford: Clarendon Press, 1981.

Cercignani subjects the work of Kökeritz (no. 85) to severe criticism, proposing that Shakespeare's pronunciation was more different from present standards of pronunciation than Kökeritz allows; he regards him as weak in his handling of evidence, specifically challenging his disregard of evidence from the writings on language of Shakespeare's contemporaries and his identification of homophonic puns. Stating that "the types of speech reflected in Shakespeare's works and in those of contemporary writers on orthography and pronunciation reveal considerable discrepancies between Elizabethan and present-day usage, although some of the older features survive, along with numerous historical variants, in modern dialects and in regional varieties of English" (28), Cercignani undertakes a fresh evaluation of the evidence. After a chapter on accentuation, he presents individual studies of short vowels, long vowels, diphthongs, unaccented vowels, and consonants.

81. Colaianni, Louis. *Shakespeare's Names: A New Pronouncing Dictionary.* New York: Quite Specific Media Group Ltd., 1999.

Colaianni "provides ... pronunciations of the names in Shakespeare's plays and poems which are both aesthetically suitable to the texts in which they occur, and mindful of the current trends in American and British pronunciation" (11); he regards the dictionary as pragmatically descriptive and not prescriptive. Names are listed alphabetically for each work and are glossed in "General American" and (English) "Received Pronunciation" except in cases where the two are identical; each pronunciation is represented in the International Phonetic Alphabet and in the Simplified Phonics Alphabet. This work is designed to replace Helge Kökeritz, *Shakespeare's Names: A Pronouncing Dictionary* (see no. 85), which Colaianni considers incomplete and out of date.

82. Dent, R. W. *Shakespeare's Proverbial Language.* Berkeley and Los Angeles: Univ. of California Press, 1981.

Dent revises and expands the "Shakespeare Index" in Tilley's *Dictionary* (no. 94). In his introduction, Dent questions Tilley's principles of inclusion and examines their consequences; without himself defining "proverb," Dent challenges the status of many of Tilley's listings. Dent's index is a list of numerical citations of locations of proverbs in Shakespeare's works; it consists of 4,684 entries, compared to 2,905 in Tilley, and omits 536 of Tilley's entries. Appendix A lists all the proverbs in the index according to the Tilley numbering, followed by the Shakespeare references. Appendix B is a list of phrases in Shakespeare that do not appear in Tilley but that Dent considers to be as legitimately called proverbial as entries in appendix A. Appendix C lists Dent's exclusions from Tilley's "Shakespeare Index." The bibliography cites the dictionaries and proverb collections that Dent used. See nos. 90, 94.

83. Dobson, E. J. *English Pronunciation 1500–1700.* 2 vols. Oxford: Clarendon Press, 1957. 2nd edition, 1968.

In vol. 1 Dobson surveys the sources of information: the writings of sixteenth- and seventeenth-century spelling reformers and of seventeenth-century phoneticians, grammars and spelling-books, grammars of foreign languages and interlingual dictionaries, books on shorthand systems, lists of "homophones," and rhyming dictionaries. Vol. 2 is devoted entirely to an extensive study of phonology based on the historical documents: Dobson discusses changes in stress and pronunciation and variations in both; he notes that in many words there was uncertainty about the placing of stress.

84. Edelman, Charles. *Shakespeare's Military Language: A Dictionary.* London and New Brunswick, N.J.: Athlone Press, 2000.

Edelman proposes that Shakespeare "did indeed possess an extraordinarily detailed knowledge of warfare, both ancient and modern" (1) and that his audience was similarly well informed. He glosses individual words and phrases by reference to historical documents, explaining their function in particular plays and poems. Entries are of various lengths and include studies of words such as "alarum," "herald," "kern," "mine," "petar/petard," "siege," "soldiers' pay," and "surgeon." Boldface type indicates a

LANGUAGE AND LINGUISTICS 41

cross-reference to another entry. Each entry concludes with references to sources in the extensive bibliography. The index is in three parts: first, an alphabetical list of Shakespeare's works and the terms in the *Dictionary* that appear in each; second, a similar list for non-Shakespearean works cited; and finally a list of historical persons named within the *Dictionary*.

85. Kökeritz, Helge. *Shakespeare's Pronunciation.* New Haven: Yale Univ. Press, 1953.

Kökeritz presents an "uptodate, comprehensive account of Shakespeare's pronunciation" (v), arguing that it differed less from current pronunciation than is usually assumed. After a discussion of the sources for evidence, he offers a detailed review of jingles and homonymic puns and an analysis of stressed vowels and diphthongs, unstressed vowels, common suffixes, consonants, and the incidence of stress. He concludes with phonetic transcriptions of five sonnets and selected passages from the plays, followed by three appendixes: on "Syncopated Words in Shakespeare," on "Shakespearean Accentuation," and "An Index of Shakespeare's Rhymes." Cercignani challenges Kökeritz's methods and conclusions (see no. 80). In *Shakespeare's Names: A Pronouncing Dictionary* (New Haven: Yale Univ. Press, 1959), a supplement to *Shakespeare's Pronunciation*, Kökeritz provides phonetic transcriptions for proper names that occur in the works; he indicates variations between British and American English, and also gives an Elizabethan pronunciation where it may have differed significantly. The introduction includes a discussion of the pronunciation of classical, Italian, and French names, and of the variant possibilities in some others. See also no. 81.

86. Onions, C. T. *A Shakespeare Glossary.* Oxford: Clarendon Press, 1911. 2nd edition, 1919. 3rd edition enlarged and revised by Robert D. Eagleson. Oxford: Clarendon Press, 1986.

See no. 23.

87. Partridge, Eric. *Shakespeare's Bawdy: A Literary and Psychological Essay and a Comprehensive Glossary.* London: Routledge and Kegan Paul, 1947. New Popular edition (revised), 1955. 3rd edition, revised and enlarged, 1968. 3rd edition, reprinted with foreword by Stanley Wells, London and New York: Routledge, 1990.

Partridge presents an extensive glossary of words with sexual or scatological reference; he cross-references fully and is sensitive to metaphors, puns, and euphemisms, but primarily in relation to heterosexual activity; he illustrates his definitions from the works and includes etymologies frequently. An introductory essay, entitled "The Sexual: The Homosexual: and Non-Sexual Bawdy in Shakespeare," precedes the glossary. In it Partridge discusses bawdy in general in Shakespeare: he constructs an author whose language suggests that he was little interested in scatology and homosexuality and very interested in women's bodies and heterosexual intercourse. The essay includes classifications of words for male and female genitals, for sexual intercourse, and for prostitutes and bawds; he also discusses the significance of patterns of imagery used for sexual matters. In the revised and enlarged edition of 1968 he corrects some errors and adds some references, especially to *Sonnets* and *Measure*. Stanley Wells's brief foreword to the 1990 reprint places Partridge's work in a historical context, assesses its strengths and limitations, and comments on the contributions of later scholars (Colman and Rubinstein, see no. 88) to the subject.

88. Rubinstein, Frankie. *A Dictionary of Shakespeare's Sexual Puns and their Significance.* Basingstoke, U.K.: Macmillan, 1984. 2nd edition, 1989.

Rubinstein's dictionary identifies numerous puns previously noted and many unnoted; she amplifies the references in Partridge (no. 87) and E. A. M. Colman (*The Dramatic Use of Bawdy in Shakespeare* [London: Longman, 1974]) to male and female homosexuality, castration, and scatology. Her entries cite other dictionaries, contemporary and recent, and make cross-references to other texts for confirmation; they include extensive explanations of the workings of the puns. Rubinstein appends an "Index to Characters" in which punning words particularly associated with a character are cited. The second edition adds a supplement that enlarges and corrects entries and adds new information specifically relating to the *Sonnets* and to similar references in Shakespeare's contemporaries and in classical literature well known in his time.

89. Schmidt, Alexander. *Shakespeare-Lexikon.* 2 vols. Berlin: Georg Reimer, 1874–75. 3rd edition revised and enlarged by Gregor Sarrazin, Berlin: Georg Reimer; New York: Stechert, 1902. 3rd edition repr. New York: Dover Publications, 1971.

Schmidt lists and defines a wide range of words used in the works, not just the "obsolete and unintelligible." He illustrates each entry with quotations from the works and occasionally from contemporary authors; he does not supply etymologies. Vol. 2 contains the following appendixes: "Grammatical Observations"; "Provincialisms"; "Words and sentences taken from foreign languages"; "List of the words forming the latter part in compositions." The third edition includes a supplement, "A Selection of New Renderings and Interpretations," in which the material of the dictionary is updated. Schmidt's *Lexikon* gives more citations from the texts

LANGUAGE AND LINGUISTICS   43

than Onions's briefer *Glossary* (no. 23); like the latter, it must be supplemented for sexual references by consulting Partridge (no. 87), Rubinstein (no. 88), and Williams (nos. 95, 96).

90. Smith, Charles G. *Shakespeare's Proverb Lore.* Cambridge: Harvard Univ. Press, 1963.

Smith supplements the work of Tilley (no. 94) in relation to Shakespeare by identifying passages in the works that derive from Latin proverbs appearing in two books used generally in Elizabethan schools, the *Sententiae Pueriles* of Leonard Culman and the *Sententiae* of Publilius Syrus. Smith cites 346 proverbs, giving the locations in Shakespeare's works, the form in either source or both, references to other classical authors from whom Shakespeare may have derived his knowledge, and citations to Tilley and other modern scholars who recorded the proverb previously. He provides a distributive index for the individual Shakespeare works and word indexes for both the Latin and English forms of the proverbs. See nos. 82, 94.

91. Sokol, B. J., and Mary Sokol. *Shakespeare's Legal Language: A Dictionary.* London: Athlone Press, 2000.

Arguing in their introduction for Shakespeare's precise interest in the law, Sokol and Sokol present a series of explanations of the legal terms that he uses, in the plays rather than in the poems. Although some entries consist of a brief paragraph or a simple cross-reference, the majority are lengthy exploratory essays on specific subjects in three parts: an initial definition of a term with an exposition of the law and its history is followed by a discussion of its relevance to particular Shakespearean texts; a detailed bibliography concludes each entry. There are substantial essays on "appeal," "bastard/bastardy," "dowager/widow," "dower/dowry," "marriage," "pre-contract," "rape," and "witch/witchcraft," for instance. Boldface type indicates a cross-reference to another entry. The bibliography of sources cited is extensive. There are two indexes: the first, "Shakespeare Passages, Scenes, Works," gives references to the texts of the works followed by the term under which the passage is discussed; the second, "Legal Terms and Concepts," identifies the sections of the dictionary under which specific terms or concepts are discussed.

92. Spevack, Marvin. *A Complete and Systematic Concordance to the Works of Shakespeare.* 9 vols. Hildesheim, Germany: Georg Olms, 1968–80.

Spevack produces a series of concordances based on the text of *The Riverside Shakespeare* (no. 2) that enable various kinds of search. Vols. 1–3 provide concordances to the plays individually in the order in which they were printed in the First Folio; the nondramatic works appear after the histories in vol. 2, and *Pericles*, *Kinsmen*, and the Hand D portion of *More* after the tragedies in vol. 3. After each play there is a concordance of the language of each speaking role in the play. Each of these concordances is preceded by relevant statistical information: the total number of speeches in a play or role, the number of lines, the total of words, with each of these categories further distributed according to the number in prose, verse, or mixed prose and verse; there is also a count of the number of different words. Vols. 4–6 print an alphabetical concordance of the complete works. Vol. 6 adds a series of appendixes: "A Word Frequency Index"; "A Reverse Word Index"; three "Indexes of Hyphenated Words" organized according to the first, second, or third component of the compound word; a list of homographs; and a conversion table to Folio TLN. Vol. 7 presents a concordance of all the stage directions and speech headings, all in old spelling. The stage directions are organized in three concordances: sequentially within each play; alphabetically in each play; and alphabetically for the complete works. They incorporate data from the First Folio and from all the quartos published before the First Folio with the addition of *Kinsmen*, the Hand D portion of *More*, Q2 *Othello*, *A Shrew*, and *The Troublesome Reign of King John*. The speech headings are organized by play as they appear in the First Folio and in all the first and copy-text quartos. Speech headings in Bad Quartos are listed separately. A second concordance lists speech headings in each play by speaking role. Vol. 8 is devoted entirely to concordances of each of the Bad Quartos—Q1 *Merry Wives*, Q1 *Henry V*, *Contention*, *True Tragedy*, Q1 *Romeo*, and Q1 *Hamlet*—and *A Shrew* and *The Troublesome Reign of King John*; followed by a concordance of all of them together and "A Word Frequency Index." Vol. 9 consists of a concordance of all substantive variants, all those instances in which *The Riverside Shakespeare* (no. 2) departs from the chosen copy-text. *The Harvard Concordance to Shakespeare* (no. 26) is a one-volume version of this concordance.

93. Spevack, Marvin. *A Shakespeare Thesaurus*. Hildesheim, Germany: Georg Olms, 1993.

Spevack organizes Shakespeare's vocabulary under categories: groups of related words concerning things or concepts are gathered and numbered so that they represent a construction of Shakespeare's idiolect. The main thesaurus contains 37 major categories, such as "health.medicine," "communication," and "motion," with 897 subgroups, such as "sickness," "malapropism," and "chase"; there are separate categories for "names: persons and places" and for "names: fictional characters." An index traces all entries in the thesaurus. All spelling and any numerical textual references

LANGUAGE AND LINGUISTICS 45

are derived from the text of *The Riverside Shakespeare* (no. 2) and refer to its related concordances. In his introduction Spevack discusses at length the structural and interpretive issues that he confronted and acknowledges that his "system is unabashedly eclectic" (ix). He explains and illustrates the problems of definition: he cites instances in which the OED, the *Shakespeare-Lexikon* (no. 89), and the *Shakespeare Glossary* (no. 23) differ in interpretation, and he discusses the challenges of, for example, obsolescent meanings, coined compounds, and figurative and transferred uses.

94. Tilley, Morris Palmer. *A Dictionary of the Proverbs in England in the Sixteenth and Seventeenth Centuries*. Ann Arbor: Univ. of Michigan Press, 1950.

Tilley presents a compilation of 11,780 proverbs, proverbial phrases, and proverbial similes found in writings of the period 1500–1700. Each proverb is listed under a catchword, usually the first substantive of the expression; proverbs are assigned a "numbering" (the initial letter of the catchword and a number) and ordered alphabetically by catchword. Each is followed by a citation of sources, with separate attention given to instances from the Shakespeare texts. The bibliography provides a full record of the sources consulted. A "Shakespeare Index" gives precise references to the location of proverbs in individual Shakespeare's works with the relevant numberings. An "Index of Significant Words" lists important words in the entry form of each proverb with the relevant numberings. See also F. P. Wilson, "The Proverbial Wisdom of Shakespeare" in F. P. Wilson, *Shakespearian and Other Studies*, ed. Helen Gardner, 142–75 (Oxford: Clarendon Press, 1969). Wilson states and illustrates by examples three ways in which Tilley's *Dictionary* needs to be supplemented: the citation of earlier occurrences of a proverb than Tilley records; other examples in Shakespeare's works than Tilley cites; and proverbs occurring in Shakespeare that Tilley does not include. Wilson concludes with an appendix in which he gives earlier examples of some of the proverbs for which Tilley's earliest citation is from Shakespeare. See also nos. 82, 90.

95. Williams, Gordon. *A Dictionary of Sexual Language and Imagery in Shakespearean and Stuart Literature*. 3 vols. London and Atlantic Highlands, N.J.: Athlone Press, 1994.

In this comprehensive dictionary of the "recurrent and shifting linguistic patterns over a period of two centuries" Williams draws on diverse print and manuscript sources—poems, plays, narratives, broadsides, pamphlets, newsbooks, travel books, memoirs, etc.—all of which are listed in his bibliography. Each entry, word or phrase, is followed by an exploratory essay, from a few lines to a few pages in length, in which he discusses numerous examples of its use; essays are in one or more parts, according to the multiplicity of ascribed meanings. He traces etymologies for many entries; citations of pre-Shakespearean uses are frequent, as are analogous occurrences in foreign sources. The majority of the evidence is derived from the latter half of the seventeenth century; Williams illustrates many entries with citations and analogues from later periods.

96. Williams, Gordon. *A Glossary of Shakespeare's Sexual Language.* London: Athlone Press, 1997.

Williams presents a comprehensive set of notes on words and phrases in Shakespeare's works, citing references and cross-references within the works, supporting his interpretations from the works of other writers of the period, and discriminating carefully between confident glossing and apt speculation. His base text is the 1986 Oxford *Complete Works*; he includes references to words occurring in the Bad Quartos. In his introduction he observes that this *Glossary* is supplementary to his earlier *Dictionary* (no. 95), focusing as it does on the personal vocabulary and distinctive practice of Shakespeare; and he supplies a narrative of the history of the glossing of sexual references in earlier scholarship, praising the work of Eric Partridge (no. 87) as foundational.

See also nos. 71, 122, 123, 124, 127, 128, 251.

C. Grammar and Rhetoric.

97. Abbott, E. A. *A Shakespearian Grammar: An Attempt to Illustrate Some of the Differences Between Elizabethan and Modern English.* 3rd edition. London: Macmillan, 1870. Repr. New York: Dover Publications, 1966.

Originally conceived as a textbook for secondary schools, Abbott's *Grammar* aims to be "a complete book of reference for all difficulties of Shakespearian syntax or prosody" (xxi). In a series of numbered "paragraphs" Abbott describes systematically and in great detail the distinctive features of Shakespeare's syntax, citing illustrative passages from the works and also from the writings of his contemporaries. He makes clear the flexibility and variety of Shakespeare's usage, documenting particularly: the substitution of parts of speech (functional shift—for instance, adjectives used as adverbs and nouns); the range of functions of many prepositions; the customary uses of pronouns, personal (especially thou/you), relative, and interrogative; the forms of verbs, especially discriminating uses of verb moods and of auxiliary verbs (shall/will, should/would, etc.); and irregularities, including transpositions in word order. His study of prosody presents a set of basic rules for the scansion of Shakespeare's verse and deals with common contractions and also words in which the accent is variable. The book concludes with an elementary discussion of the nature of simile, metaphor, and personification that includes examples of "bad" metaphors and personifications from Shakespeare's plays. There is an index to the quotations from the plays (but not from the poems) and a verbal index of subjects and individual words discussed. Blake (no. 71) discusses the limitations of Abbott's work, noting its incompleteness by current standards and stating that "[n]o attempt is made to provide a description of Shakespeare's language on its own terms since the focus is always on what is different" from Modern English (169).

98. Burton, Dolores M. *Shakespeare's Grammatical Style.* Austin: Texas Univ. Press, 1974.

As a model for quantitative stylistic analysis Burton pursues features of *Richard II* and *Antony* as a means of locating or determining distinctive qualities of the linguistic style of each play. In place of the customary study of imagery and vocabulary she addresses the contribution of grammar and syntax to meaning. Using the two plays as works characteristic of different periods of Shakespeare's career, she examines, for example, displaying her evidence in explanatory statistical charts, the relative occurrence and the circumstances of the occurrence of "wh- clauses"; the relative length of sentences; the relative proportions of paratactic and hypotactic constructions; aspects of deviant word order; and the distribution of determiners (definite, demonstrative, and possessive) before specific nouns, titles, and proper names. Her objective is the comprehensive description of the details that constitute the particular verbal objects and from that the interpretation of the texts. Appendix A presents "Supplementary Tables and Notes on Procedures"; they include further studies, with charts and lists, of interrogatives and imperatives in both plays, including their proportional occurrence in the roles of the main characters; of kinds of adjectival suffixes (English or Latinate); of sentence structures; and of distinctive features of the vocabulary of individual characters.

99. Cusack, Bridget. "Shakespeare and the Tune of the Time." *Shakespeare Survey* 23 (1970): 1–12. Repr. in Salmon and Burness (no. 79).

Cusack discusses the incidence of newer and older linguistic forms in Shakespeare, distinguishing mere alternative usages from those where discriminations of register of speech are made. She examines instances of "-eth" and "-es" in the third person singular present tense, of negatives using "do" and those in the form "verb+not," and of "do" as an indicator of formality or a means of emphasis; the employment of archaic forms and neologisms in relation to characters' speech habits, including arch and fashionable uses, but also for metrical convenience; examples of puns based on two available meanings of a word whose meaning is shifting; words for which two stress-patterns may exist, or in which the option of suppressing or pronouncing a syllable is present; and modes of greeting.

100. Ewbank, Inga-Stina. "Shakespeare and the arts of language." In *The Cambridge Companion to Shakespeare Studies*, ed. Stanley Wells, 49–66. Cambridge: Cambridge Univ. Press, 1986. Repr., 1991.

Ewbank places Shakespeare in the context of an age preoccupied with the power of the arts of language and demonstrates how he employed and developed those arts in his work. After discussing the self-reflectiveness and the variety of his use of language in *Tempest*, she explores his "moulding" (56) of language, his exploitation of functional shift (making of verbs out of nouns, for example), his addition of prefixes to words (particularly "un-" to verbs), and his creation of compound words. She demonstrates further his exploration of rhetorical figures and their integration into dramatic structures and his skill in the use of tropes, particularly metaphor. She includes numerous illustrations from the texts, and her examinations of their workings are both detailed and precise.

101. Houston, John Porter. *Shakespearean Sentences: A Study in Style and Syntax*. Baton Rouge: Louisiana State Univ. Press, 1988.

Houston examines the characteristic patterns of sentences in the blank verse of the plays and their usefulness for the interpretation of the plays and of the construction of character. He examines the various forms that subject-verb-object relations take, the incidence of hypotactic and paratactic structures, the presence and absence of conjunctions (polysyndeton and asyndeton), the use of parentheses and of disruptive syntax. Emphasizing the rhetorical foundations of Shakespeare's art, and attending particularly to the modes of creating heightened and colloquial styles, he illustrates his points by studies of the distinctive features of the sentences of individual plays.

102. Joseph, Sister Miriam, C.S.C. *Shakespeare's Use of the Arts of Language*. New York: Hafner, 1947.

Sister Miriam Joseph argues that Shakespeare's habits of writing were founded on the training in logic and rhetoric in the schools of his time. After a summary of the Tudor educational curriculum, she initially surveys the current general theory of composition, establishing its basis in the relations of grammar, logic, and rhetoric. She then demonstrates how

Shakespeare's verbal inventiveness and expressive power derive from his imaginative exploitation of the forms and figures prescribed by rhetorical theorists; she suggests in her numerous illustrations how he achieved particular dramatic effects. The book concludes with a lengthy but succinct exposition of "the general theory of composition and reading as defined and illustrated by Tudor logicians and rhetoricians" (291-399). See also T. W. Baldwin, *William Shakspere's Small Latine and Lesse Greeke*, 2 vols. (Urbana: Univ. of Illinois Press, 1944).

103. Lanham, Richard A. *A Handlist of Rhetorical Terms*. Berkeley and Los Angeles: Univ. of California Press, 1968.

Lanham organizes this reference work in five lists. The first is a full "Alphabetical List of Terms," in which he cites and cross-references rhetorical terms in their classical forms but also in George Puttenham's Englished forms; notes or brief essays with examples explain each term. In the second he presents the "Terms Classified According to Divisions of Rhetoric." In the third, "The Terms By Type," Lanham organizes the terms by descriptive categories to enable a reader to locate the term appropriate to the verbal expression. The fourth lists "Terms Classified as Ornaments" with curt definitions, and the fifth, "Terms Especially Useful in Literary Criticism," is a selection of items from the first list with shortened definitions.

104. Magnusson, Lynne. *Shakespeare and Social Dialogue: Dramatic Language and Elizabethan Letters*. Cambridge: Cambridge Univ. Press, 1999.

Magnusson explores language in relation to forms of conversation in Shakespeare's works. Informed by ideas drawn from discourse analysis, sociolinguistics, and particularly politeness theory, she examines the language and rhetoric of Elizabethan correspondence and epistolary manuals in order to derive "a practical inventory of distinctions that will permit analysis of characters' concrete utterances as products of social intercourse" (19). On the basis of documented linguistic custom she illuminates social behavior and interaction, especially in *Henry VIII*, *Lear*, *Much Ado*, and *Othello*; she argues that Shakespeare's construction of character should be considered less in terms of the linguistic capacity of the individual and more in the light of "social and power relations" (181) as manifested in language.

105. McIntosh, Angus. "'As You Like It': A Grammatical Clue to Character." *Review of English Literature* 4 (1963): 68-81. Repr. in *Patterns of Language*, ed. Angus McIntosh and M. A. K. Halliday, 70-82. Bloomington: Indiana Univ. Press, 1963.

McIntosh explores the use of "thou/you" in the conversations of Rosalind and Celia to establish that the selection of pronouns of address was not simply determined by levels of social rank or generalized conditions of intimate relationship, but also occasioned by the "expression of transient attitudes" (68). McIntosh shows how the pronouns of address in these two speakers are not always consistent within even short speeches or in the course of scenes, and how the process of the play includes both the relative reversal of their initial customary modes of address and the representation of their later loss of intimacy by the abandonment of the "thou" form.

106. **Mulholland, Joan.** "'Thou' and 'You' in Shakespeare: A Study in the Second Person Pronoun." *English Studies* 48 (1967): 34–43. Repr. in Salmon and Burness (no. 79).

Using *Much Ado* and *Lear* as the sources of her observations, Mulholland summarizes the frequencies and circumstances of occurrence of "th-" and "you" forms and concludes that there are no clear grammatical reasons for variations. Extending the work of McIntosh (no. 105) she examines speech habits within four different social classes, and within each of men speaking to men, men to women, women to men, and women to women. Her tentative conclusion is that "you" is the form commonly used among the upper class, apart from between father and daughter, and also of women to their female servants.

107. **Partridge, A. C.** *Orthography in Shakespeare and Elizabethan Drama.* Lincoln: Univ. of Nebraska Press, 1964.

Partridge presents a series of related studies of colloquial contractions, elision, prosody, and punctuation. He surveys the evidence for contractions in late sixteenth century writing from manuscript playbooks, including *More*. He discusses distinctive features of Shakespeare's orthography in *Venus and Adonis* and other printed texts, but he is aware of the degree to which in relation both to punctuation and spelling in quarto and Folio the hands of scribe or compositor may be an intervening presence.

108. **Platt, Peter G.** "Shakespeare and Rhetorical Culture." In *A Companion to Shakespeare*, ed. David Scott Kastan (no. 22), 277–96. Oxford: Blackwell, 1999.

After asserting the importance of rhetoric in Shakespeare's time, Platt first presents a survey of the classical tradition of rhetoric, discussing the contributions of Aristotle and Cicero particularly to both the structure of eloquence in discourse and the pursuit of knowledge. He then proceeds to discuss the way in which rhetoric was conceived in the Early Modern period as an instrument in self-presentation and self-fashioning. Having drawn attention to Shakespeare's awareness of this figure of the protean rhetorical being in his creation of Richard of Gloucester (*3 Henry VI*), Platt concludes with an examination of a passage from *Merchant* in which he demonstrates Shakespeare's acknowledgment of the duality of rhetoric, its power both to distort and to civilize.

109. Quirk, Randolph. "Shakespeare and the English Language." In *A New Companion to Shakespeare Studies*, ed. Kenneth Muir and S. Schoenbaum, 67–82. Cambridge: Cambridge Univ. Press, 1971. Repr. in Salmon and Burness (no. 79).

Quirk addresses the relation of Shakespeare's usage to the language of the time; he concentrates primarily on grammar and vocabulary. With respect to the former he discusses the distinction of "thou" and "you" as marked and unmarked forms, the significance of "thou" and "thee" after imperative verbs, and the use of "do" as an auxiliary to confer weight and sonority to phrases; with respect to the latter, he reviews instances of strange words and deceptively familiar words, the fashion for invention of vocabulary and Shakespeare's habits of word-formation, and lexical patterning in the texts.

110. Salmon, Vivian. "Sentence Structure in Colloquial Shakespearian English." In *Transactions of the Philological Society, 1965*, 105–40. Repr. in Salmon and Burness (no. 79).

Noting that dramatic texts are a rare source of evidence for the forms of Elizabethan colloquial speech, Salmon uses prose passages from *Merry Wives*, *1 Henry IV*, *2 Henry IV*, and *Henry V* as the basis of an enquiry into the syntax of statements, yes/no questions, "wh-" questions, exclamations, commands, and question tags. A table presents the range of syntactical options available, and the discussion illustrates the kinds of selections made by speakers in the plays. Salmon states that the wide range of available syntactical structures is an "outstanding feature" (135) of Elizabethan English; her discussion illuminates, for example, the significance of the various uses of "do" with the verb, the structures of sentences beginning with various adverbs and conjunctions, and levels of politeness and brusqueness implicit in forms of command.

111. Salmon, Vivian. "Some Functions of Shakespearian Word-Formation." *Shakespeare Survey* 23 (1970): 13–26. Repr. in Salmon and Burness (no. 79).

Postulating initially that Shakespeare's coining of words was a response to grammatical, phonetic, and syntactic needs, Salmon reviews the ways in which he used suffixes ("-ment," "-ure," "-ing," "-ive") to create neologisms and proposes, with illustrations, that many of the neologisms were coined for metrical reasons: "To avoid the juxtaposition of two heavy stresses" (16); "To eliminate superfluous unstressed syllables" (17); "To ensure coincidence of metrical and lexical stress" (18). Acknowledging that metrical necessity as occasion of coining is a characteristic of the earlier works, she then discusses the exploitation of neologisms for rhetorical effect and for the creation of character and setting and analyzes the structure of various compound epithets and nouns. Lastly, she examines the features of Shakespeare's formation of verbs, noting the use of the prefixes "dis-" and "un-," the creation of compound verbs, and the conversion of nouns and adjectives into verbs.

112. Salmon, Vivian. "The Spelling and Punctuation of Shakespeare's Time." In William Shakespeare, *The Complete Works*. Original-Spelling edition. Stanley Wells and Gary Taylor, general eds., xliii–lvi. Oxford: Clarendon Press, 1986.

Salmon provides initially a brief history of English spelling, in which she describes the development of consistent practices in the seventeenth century and explains differences between modern spelling and that of the period of Shakespeare's texts, including the use of double consonants, the incidence of final "e," and the uses of i/j, u/v, and ie/y. She then discusses three kinds of differences of spelling of individual words: those due to scribal convention, those that reflect a difference in pronunciation, and those where the earlier spelling represents more faithfully than the present an unchanged pronunciation. Asserting that the habits of scribes and compositors obscure and overlie Shakespeare's own orthography, she argues that texts such as those quartos believed to be printed from his manuscripts are most likely to preserve his distinctive forms, particularly in elisions and syncopated forms, in passages in foreign languages, and in dialect words; she presents evidence to suggest that the spellings "somnet" (for "summit") and "culd" (for "culled") are his idiosyncratic forms. Salmon concludes with a brief history and discussion of the conventions of punctuation in the period, notes the variant practices of compositors, who assumed responsibility for punctuating the text, and after reviewing features of the surviving Shakespeare texts asserts that few specific interpretive conclusions concerning Shakespeare's practices can be drawn from them.

113. Smithers, G. V. "Guide-lines for Interpreting the Use of the Suffix '-ed' in Shakespeare's English." *Shakespeare Survey* 23 (1970): 27–37.

Smithers notes that the suffix "-ed" derives both from the form of the past participle of verbs and also from an Old English suffix that changes nouns to adjectives with the sense "provided or endowed with, having, having the quality of." He examines various examples of formations of the second kind, showing particularly how with nouns the suffix functions similarly to "-ful," but also how Shakespeare used the suffix with verbs as well to produce meanings equivalent to modern "-ing" and "-able." In the course of his argument he illuminates a number of problematic words in the plays.

114. Trousdale, Marion. *Shakespeare and the Rhetoricians.* Chapel Hill: Univ. of North Carolina Press, 1982.

In examining the presence of Elizabethan rhetorical practice in Shakespeare's works, Trousdale advances a theory of their composition and structure, particularly concentrating on the distinction between things and words. Arguing against a theory of the work's organic wholeness, she proposes that in following the teachings of Erasmus and other Tudor rhetoricians such as Richard Rainolde, Thomas Wilson, Henry Peachum, and George Puttenham, Shakespeare aims to unfold ideas rather than to discover them, his verbal development is in the service of pattern rather than of character, and his use of figures of ornament is a function of artistic display rather than of the establishment of meaning. See also Jane Donawerth, *Shakespeare and the Sixteenth-Century Study of Language* (Urbana: Univ. of Illinois Press, 1984).

115. Vickers, Brian. "Shakespeare's Use of Rhetoric." In *A New Companion to Shakespeare Studies*, ed. Kenneth Muir and S. Schoenbaum, 83–98. Cambridge: Cambridge Univ. Press, 1971. Repr. in Salmon and Burness (no. 79).

Vickers initially presents a brief history of rhetoric. After establishing the primacy of *elocutio* for the dramatist, he makes clear the distinction between tropes and figures or schemes and then provides a concise series of definitions (with examples from the plays) of the most frequently occurring figures. The last section deals with Shakespeare's exploitation of rhetorical figures. Vickers explains how the rhetoricians believed that specific figures represented and expressed states of mind or feelings; on this foundation he then shows how Shakespeare used the figures, adapting them to his needs in the plays. He concludes with a study of passages from *Richard III*, *Othello*, and *Winter's Tale* in which he shows the relative stiffness of his practice in *Richard III* and the comparative flexibility of the later verse; he argues that Shakespeare had internalized the structures of rhetoric to produce a language more capable of expressing feeling.

See also nos. 69, 70, 71, 72, 73, 74, 75, 76, 77, 78, 79, 116, 119, 198, 199, 200, 201, 202, 203, 204, 205, 244, 256, 262.

D. Verse and Prose.

116. Barish, Jonas A. *Ben Jonson and the Language of Prose Comedy.* Cambridge: Harvard Univ. Press, 1960.

In chapter 1, "Antecedents," Barish provides a background to his study of Ben Jonson's prose, reviewing the distinctive features of the prose of Gascoigne's *Supposes*, the plays of Lyly, *The Famous Victories of Henry the Fifth*, and the plays of Shakespeare. He discerns logicality as a characteristic quality of Shakespeare's prose; he describes certain features as distinctive, including the organization of ideas into antithetical structures, the establishment of cause and effect relations, the placing of the dependent clause before the major clause, and the exploitation of symmetry and exact balance. In chapter 2, "Prose as Prose," he discusses other examples of Shakespeare's prose that resemble Jonson's "curt style" in their brevity and lack of conjunctions, but suggests that even they retain some element of regularity of rhythm and proportion. See also Jonas A. Barish, "Continuities and Discontinuities in Shakespearian Prose" (in *Shakespeare 1971: Proceedings of the World Shakespeare Congress, Vancouver, August 1971*, ed. Clifford Leech and J. M. R. Margeson, 59–75. Toronto: Univ. of Toronto Press, 1972). Following and modifying the views of Henry W. Wells in "The Continuity of Shakesperian Prose" (*The Shakespeare Association Bulletin* 15 [1940], 175–83), Barish argues, providing numerous illustrations, that Shakespeare developed a distinctive mature prose style early and that it did not undergo the kind of development and change that is apparent in his verse, although there is a reduction of conspicuous word-play and an increased tightness of expression in his later writing.

117. Crane, Milton. *Shakespeare's Prose.* Chicago: Univ. of Chicago Press, 1951.

After a survey of the use of prose in plays by Shakespeare's contemporaries Lyly, Marlowe, Kyd, Jonson, Beaumont and Fletcher, Middleton, Webster, and Ford, Crane presents a summary of the functions of prose as a contrast to verse in Shakespeare's plays. His systematic play-by-play review concentrates upon its appearance, for instance, in the language of characters of low rank, in subplots, and in comic scenes and satirical speeches; he also attends to the significance of its occurrence in particular roles, especially Falstaff and Hamlet. His method is classificatory rather than analytical, since he devotes no attention to syntactic structure.

118. Ness, F. W. *The Use of Rhyme in Shakespeare's Plays.* New Haven: Yale Univ. Press, 1941.

Ness examines the occurrence of rhyme in the plays, reviewing initially the contexts in which Shakespeare employs it: at the ends of scenes and acts (the most frequent use), at the ends of speeches, for the entrances and exits of characters, in prologues and epilogues, for *sententiae*, song, doggerel, etc. He notes that rhyme is characteristic of the earlier plays rather than the later, and attributes the decline in its use in the course of Shakespeare's career to a reduction in his desire for its particular effects, suggesting that its restraints were not congenial to the greater freedom that he exercised in later composition. In an appendix Ness lists by act, scene, and line all the rhymes (except those in songs) in Shakespeare's plays according to the categories of use established in the study.

119. Vickers, Brian. *The Artistry of Shakespeare's Prose*. London: Methuen, 1968.

Vickers discriminates in chapter 1 the characteristic circumstances in which Shakespeare usually employs prose—in letters and pronouncements, and in the creation of characters of lower rank, of drunks, and of madmen. In chapter 2 he then explains his critical approach, which entails an examination of the imagery, the patterns of the sentence structures, and the use of rhetorical figures. In a chronological sequence of studies encompassing nearly all the plays, he then describes Shakespeare's development in the exploitation of prose; he presents detailed textual examinations, including precise diagrams of sentence structures, to illustrate Shakespeare's use of syntactic and rhetorical devices to create dramatic character.

120. Wright, George T. *Shakespeare's Metrical Art*. Berkeley and Los Angeles: Univ. of California Press, 1988.

Wright presents a thorough and extensive study of Shakespearean metrics, providing at every stage a wealth of illustrative examples. Beginning with a survey of uses of the iambic pentameter line in Chaucer, Lydgate, Sidney, and others, he examines the metrical characteristics of verse in the *Sonnets* and the plays; he devotes chapters to short and shared lines, long lines, ambiguous syllabification (compressions and expansions), lines with missing and extra syllables, the incidence of trochees, the relation of phrase to line. In later chapters he discusses Shakespeare's exploitation of variations in his dramatic verse and the effects that they produce in the shaping of speeches—the play of the structured sentence within the long speech—and particularly in characterization. He concludes by considering the metrical habits of Donne and Milton and placing Shakespeare in the history of the use of blank verse. Elsewhere Wright presents brief studies of Shakespeare's metrical technique: "Shakespeare's Poetic Techniques," in *William Shakespeare: His World, His Work, His Influence*, ed.

John F. Andrews, 3 vols., 2: 363-87 (no. 68); and "Hearing Shakespeare's Dramatic Verse," in *A Companion to Shakespeare*, ed. David Scott Kastan (no. 235), 256-76. See also Dorothy Sipe, *Shakespeare's Metrics* (New Haven and London: Yale Univ. Press, 1968), who argues from the occurrence of syllabic variants in synonyms (bide/abide, quite/quittance/requite as verbs) that "Shakespeare wrote carefully constructed iambic verse into which he introduced only those few minor variations considered permissible in his time" (vii); and Marina Tarlinskaja, *Shakespeare's Verse: Iambic Pentameter and the Poet's Idiosyncrasies* (American University Studies, series 4—English Language and Literature, vol. 41. New York: Peter Lang, 1987), a technical linguistic study of Shakespeare's verse.

See also nos. 68, 72, 75, 76, 77, 78, 79, 80, 81, 85, 97, 111.

E. Vocabulary and Imagery.

121. Armstrong, Edward A. *Shakespeare's Imagination*. London: Lindsay Drummond, 1946. Revised edition, Lincoln: Univ. of Nebraska Press, 1963.

Armstrong's establishment of the characteristic features of Shakespeare's imagination begins from the identification of image clusters, recurrent patterns in which words that appear unrelated by topic are linked by proximity in the texts of various works; he is able to establish principles of association that are latent in them. Armstrong explores a number of clusters and provides charts of the incidence and the range of some of the more noteworthy: the kite (birds, bedding, food, death, etc.), the beetle (birds, mice, night, death, etc.), the drone and the weasel (king-creatures, mood, sucking, music, etc.), and the goose (disease, music, restraint, etc.). See no. 130.

122. Empson, William. *The Structure of Complex Words*. London: Chatto and Windus, 1951. 2nd edition, 1964.

Empson's study of modes of assigning meaning and his contribution to a method of systematic description are initially presented in two chapters entitled "Feelings in Words" and "Statements in Words." His illustrative investigations involve examinations of the histories of a number of words with examples from various periods of English life and literature. Among the focused studies are chapters concerning the complex and various meanings of specific words in Shakespeare plays: "Fool in *Lear*," "*Timon's* Dog," "Honest in *Othello*," and "Sense in *Measure for Measure*." See also Paul Jorgensen, *Redeeming Shakespeare's Words* (Berkeley and Los Angeles: Univ. of California Press, 1962), in which Jorgensen explores in a series of brief essays the variety of meanings that specific words have in particular plays, including "honesty" in *Othello*, "nothing" in *Much Ado*, "honor" in *1 Henry IV*, and "noble" in *Coriolanus*.

123. Hart, Alfred. "Vocabularies of Shakespeare's Plays" and "The Growth of Shakespeare's Vocabulary." *Review of English Studies* 19 (1943): 128–40, 242–54.

In these joint articles Hart provides statistics about the extent and distribution of Shakespeare's vocabulary. In the first, after a discussion of the problems of defining a word and a statement of his own criteria of discrimination, he produces a chart that establishes for each play and the poems the length in lines; the number of words in the work's vocabulary; the number of words peculiar to that work alone; and the percentage of peculiar words in the vocabulary of each work. He observes from his figures that the size of the vocabulary in plays increases over the course of the career; that the vocabularies of the narrative poems are relatively copious in comparison to those of the plays; and that the total of words peculiar to one work only is over 7,200, about 40 percent of the total vocabulary of the works. In the second article he describes the total vocabulary as 17,677 words; then to show that the constant inflow of fresh words in each new work is a distinctive feature of Shakespeare's language he presents a chart that displays the distribution of words that occur in between one and ten plays only.

124. Hulme, Hilda M. *Explorations in Shakespeare's Language*. London: Longman, 1962.

Working on the principle that problematic passages in the texts of the plays should be thoroughly explored before emendation is proposed, Hulme examines a large number of verbal cruxes and suggests new meanings or interpretations for about two hundred words or phrases. She derives her evidence from a wide range of sources: regional contemporary manuscript records, published works of Shakespeare's contemporaries, Latin dictionaries, proverb lore and idiom, and the specialized languages of specific social practices (such as falconry), as well as the playtexts themselves. She also uses her knowledge of variation in pronunciation and its possible relation to spelling in the earliest printed texts to exploit the resources of the OED and thus provide new identifications of difficult words; she is attentive to survivals of regional forms in the texts, particularly from Warwickshire.

125. Hulme, Hilda M. "The Spoken Language and the Dramatic Text." *Shakespeare Quarterly* 9 (1958): 379–86. Repr. in Salmon and Burness (no. 79).

Stressing the need to recognize that the Shakespeare text is designed to represent spoken language, Hulme examines a number of problematic passages, which she illuminates by reference to Elizabethan sources—a Latin dictionary, the work of John Heywood—and to Tilley (no. 94). She is particularly interested to explore situations in which one or two obscure words in the dialogue of a text may be explained as an oblique play upon an Elizabethan proverb or idiomatic phrase that is no longer current.

126. Mahood, M. M. *Shakespeare's Wordplay.* London: Methuen, 1957.

Noting the history of the criticism of Shakespeare's use of puns, Mahood discusses his exploitation of wordplay in the plays and poems. She describes how associative wordplay is the basis for the organization of speeches and dialogues and how it creates psychological character. She argues that complexes of ideas located in particular words function as structural principles in plays and illustrates this position with studies of *Romeo*, *Richard II*, *Hamlet*, *Macbeth*, and *Winter's Tale*; she devotes a chapter to the distinctive wordplay of the *Sonnets*.

127. Replogle, Carol. "Shakespeare's Salutations: A Study in Stylistic Etiquette." *Studies in Philology* 70 (1973): 172–86. Repr. in Salmon and Burness (no. 79).

Replogle discusses with reference to contemporary courtesy books and records of historical correspondence the importance to the Elizabethans of titles and their appropriate usage, especially with regard to their frequency in address. Stressing their punctiliousness in maintaining decorum she illuminates passages from the plays by observing changes in modes of address, particularly discussing their dramatic significance in *Richard II*, *1 Henry IV*, *2 Henry IV*, and *Coriolanus*.

128. Shirley, Frances Ann. *Swearing and Perjury in Shakespeare's Plays.* London: Allen and Unwin, 1979.

In interpreting the function of oaths and perjury as structural elements of the plays, Shirley discusses the language of swearing. She shows how concerned the culture of Shakespeare's day was with swearing and uses contemporary plays and also prose writings directly on the subject as evidence to establish habits in swearing, particularly to determine degrees of seriousness of particular words and phrases in casual swearing, and their relation to social rank, to profession, and to current fashion. Specifically with regard to Shakespeare's works she shows how he uses oaths as a mode of characterization, remaining aware that the texts of F-only plays dating from before 1606 may well have been modified to comply with the law; she suggests that the texts of plays written after 1606 show his compliance with the regulations.

129. Spurgeon, Caroline. *Shakespeare's Imagery and What It Tells Us.* Cambridge: Cambridge Univ. Press, 1935.

In the pursuit of detecting the identity and the "deeper thoughts" of Shakespeare from the language of the works, Spurgeon aims in part 1 to identify Shakespeare in his use of images and the areas of human knowledge and experience upon which he draws; in so doing she contrasts the categories of reference and their characteristic proportions of occurrence with those of other writers such as Bacon and Marlowe. Thus she reveals distinctive features of his language, discussing his use of words relating, for instance, to sports and games, the heavens and the sea, colors and music, animals and gardens. In part 2 she discusses the function of imagery in individual plays, noting characteristic aspects of their language patterns. The appendixes include numerous charts showing the ranges of images in specific plays and the complete works, of images in selected works of Marlowe and Bacon, and of images of daily life in Shakespeare in comparison with Marlowe, Jonson, Chapman, Dekker, and Massinger. See also Wolfgang Clemen, *The Development of Shakespeare's Imagery* (London: Methuen, 1951).

130. Whiter, Walter. *A Specimen of a Commentary on Shakespeare. Containing I. Notes on "As You Like It." II. An Attempt to Explain and Illustrate Various Passages, on a New Principle of Criticism, Derived from Mr. Locke's Doctrine of the Association of Ideas.* London, 1794.

In the *Attempt* Whiter argues that what prior critics such as Samuel Johnson criticized in Shakespeare's wordplay as a predilection for "quibbles" is rather the unconscious operation of the principle of the association of ideas; he is interested in locating in irrational collocations the distinctive unconscious operations of the creative mind. In his study, consequently, he explores numerous examples of verbal and image clusters in the works, and in so doing illuminates the details of the texts, makes the case for the retention of readings that others proposed to emend, and establishes (whether conscious or unconscious) habitual patterns of association that recur in the language of the works. See no. 121.

See also nos. 23, 47, 69, 70, 71, 72, 73, 74, 75, 76, 77, 78, 79, 84, 87, 88, 89, 91, 92, 93, 95, 96, 98, 100, 109, 111, 119, 254, 255, 256, 257, 258, 259, 260, 262, 264.

IV. TEXTUAL STUDIES

A. Resources.

1. Bibliography; Bibliographical Surveys.

131. Gaskell, Philip. *A New Introduction to Bibliography*. Oxford: Clarendon Press, 1972. Repr., with corrections, 1974.

Gaskell's work replaces the earlier standard bibliographical handbook, Ronald B. McKerrow, *An Introduction to Bibliography for Literary Students* (Oxford: Clarendon Press, 1927, 2nd impression with corrections, 1928). Gaskell gives information on all aspects of the printing process in the hand-press period with a view to providing an understanding of the transmission of texts. Separate sections deal with the nature of types, composition, paper, imposition, presswork, binding, illustration, and patterns of production; he also discusses the conduct of the book-trade in England up to 1800. After a discussion of machine-press printing, Gaskell turns to issues of bibliographical description and textual bibliography and textual criticism, addressing problems that relate to the interpetation and editing of Shakespeare texts. In the appendixes he reprints "A Note on Elizabethan Handwriting" from McKerrow's *Introduction*. The book is extensively illustrated. It includes a large reference bibliography.

132. Howard-Hill, T. H. *Shakespearian Bibliography and Textual Criticism: A Bibliography*. Oxford: Clarendon Press, 1971. 2nd edition (revised and enlarged, to 1995), Signal Mountain, Tenn.: Summertown, 2000.

The first edition is volume 2 of the *Index to British Literary Bibliography*; it presents a comprehensive bibliography of studies up to the end of 1969. The second edition is the successor to the first but not part of the series; it is enlarged to include material published in 1995. In the second edition Howard-Hill arranges his entries under five headings: "General Bibliographies of and Guides to Shakespearian Literature" (25 entries); "Shakespeare—General Bibliographies and Guides" (130 entries); "Works" ("as physical objects that can be listed, collected, counted, and eventually reissued in different editions" [xiii]) (880 entries); "Textual Studies" ("the application of bibliographical and textual analysis to the works" [xiii]) (309 entries); and "Individual Works" (1,016 entries). The section "Apocrypha" within "Individual Works" has separate entries for *More* and *Kinsmen*, but for no other works. The annotations are brief.

133. Williams, George Walton. *The Craft of Printing and the Publication of Shakespeare's Works*. Washington, D.C.: Folger Shakespeare Library, 1985.

In this short book Williams provides the basic knowledge that the student of Shakespeare needs concerning Elizabethan printing practices and their relation to the texts of Shakespeare. After a history of the invention of printing he discusses the separate aspects of printing: the structure of the press, the nature of types (their design and casting), ink, paper, the process of printing itself (composition, imposition, presswork, and proofreading), and binding. Having described the operation of the printing trade in England, he gives a brief summary of the printing of Shakespeare's works, dealing first with the poems and then describing the publication of the plays in quarto and Folio, using tables to illustrate his statements. He divides the quartos into Bad and Good, including *Richard III* 1597 and *Lear* 1608 among the former; he explains the distinctiveness of the Pavier quartos (see Greg, no. 155); and he discusses the nature of the folio editions, identifying in his tables the printer's copy for each of the First Folio texts, and describing the appearance in the Third Folio of the seven additional plays.

134. "The Year's Contributions to Shakespearean Study: Textual Studies." *Shakespeare Survey* 1–53 (1948–2000): various pages.

Each volume contains an extensive survey of recent textual scholarship, including newly published editions. With vol. 37 the subtitle changed to "Editions and Textual Studies." The authors are: vols. 1–16, 18 James G. McManaway; there was no article in vol. 17; vols. 19–21 J. K. Walton; vols. 22–30 Richard Proudfoot; vols. 31–36 George Walton Williams; vols. 37–43 MacDonald P. Jackson; vols. 44–48 H. R. Woudhuysen; vols. 49–51 John Jowett; vols. 52–53 Eric Rasmussen.

2. Facsimiles of Quartos and Folios.

135. Allen, Michael J. B., and Kenneth Muir, eds. *Shakespeare's Plays in Quarto*. Berkeley and Los Angeles: Univ. of California Press, 1981.

Subtitled "A Facsimile Edition of Copies Primarily from the Henry E. Huntington Library," this book reproduces 22 quartos, specifically all the editions identified as First Quartos, with the Second Quartos of *Romeo* and *Hamlet*, and also *Contention* and *True Tragedy* (both from the copies in the Bodleian Library). *Titus* 1594 is reproduced from the unique

Folger Shakespeare Library copy; some pages in *Hamlet* 1603 and *Pericles* 1609 are provided from copies in the British Library. The images are actual size, printed two pages to the page. In the short introduction Allen and Muir divide the quartos into Bad and Good; they discuss some of the variant readings in different quartos of the same play, in uncorrected and corrected states of formes of the same printing of a play, and in quarto and Folio texts of the same play. In appendixes they list press variants in each quarto, provide notes on the copies used, and clarify obscured readings.

136. *The Norton Facsimile: The First Folio of Shakespeare.* Prepared by Charlton Hinman. 2nd edition, with a new introduction by Peter W. M. Blayney. New York: W. W. Norton, 1996.

The facsimile is of pages in the latest and most corrected state or else in the invariant state, selected from various exemplars in the Folger Shakespeare Library; lines of type are numbered by through line numbering (see no. 4 for fuller description). The second edition prints both Hinman's original and Blayney's new introduction; Blayney updates and corrects Hinman extensively. Blayney distinguishes Isaac Jaggard and Edward Blount as the publishers and William Jaggard as the printer; describes the production as a commercial venture for all participants, including John Heminge and Henry Condell; corrects Hinman on the economics of printing quartos, calling the First Folio the most expensive playbook ever offered, and estimating the print run as 750 rather than the 1,200 copies that Hinman posited. Blayney questions Hinman's derivation of copy from either foul papers or promptbooks, suggesting that a variety of possible sources must be assumed for printer's copy; he challenges Hinman's classifications of the quartos into Good, Doubtful, and Bad, correcting inaccurate statements and advancing more recent judgments. Concerning proofreading, Blayney revises Hinman's description of variants, corrects his description of the proofing process, following McKenzie (no. 201) in asserting that pages were proofed before printing began and that what Hinman describes is stop-press proof correction. Drawing on the work of scholars since Hinman as well as his own, Blayney summarizes the current state of knowledge concerning compositors, estimating the number working on the Folio at eight, or perhaps nine (rather than Hinman's five). He includes a table that identifies the compositor of each page and the order in which the pages were set.

137. Shakespeare Quarto Facsimiles. London: The Shakespeare Association and Sidgwick and Jackson, Limited, 1939–52 (nos. 1–8); Oxford: Clarendon Press, 1957–75 (nos. 9–16).

Sixteen quartos were reproduced in facsimile: 1. *Lear* 1608; 2. *Merchant* 1600; 3. *Merry Wives* 1602; 4. *Hamlet* 1604–5; 5. *Pericles* 1609; 6. *Romeo* 1599; 7. *Hamlet* 1603; 8. *Troilus* 1609; 9. *Henry V* 1600; 10. *Love's Labour's* 1598; 11. *Richard Duke of York* 1595 (i.e., *True Tragedy*); 12. *Richard III* 1597; 13. *Richard II* 1597; 14. *1 Henry IV* 1598; 15. *Much Ado* 1600; 16. *Othello* 1622. W. W. Greg edited nos. 1–12 and 14; Greg co-edited no. 13 with Charlton Hinman; Hinman edited nos. 15 and 16. With Oxford University Press the Malone Society has published further facsimiles of substantive or major quartos to supplement the series: *Contention* 1594, ed. William Montgomery (1985); *2 Henry IV* 1600, ed. Thomas L. Berger (1990); *Dream* 1600, ed. Thomas L. Berger (1995); *A Shrew* 1594, ed. Stephen Roy Miller (1998); *Romeo* 1597, ed. Jill L. Levenson and Barry Gaines (2000).

138. Shakespeare, William. *Sonnets 1609.* Menston, U.K.: Scolar Press, 1968.

This facsimile of a copy of the 1609 Quarto *Shake-speares Sonnets* is introduced by a brief unsigned note about the book and about the printing history of the *Sonnets* to 1780. Scolar Press printed similar facsimiles of copies of the First Quartos of *Venus and Adonis* (1593) and *Lucrece* (1594) (both Menston, 1968). A facsimile text of the 1609 *Sonnets* is reproduced opposite a modernized edited text in Stephen Booth, *Shakespeare's Sonnets* (New Haven: Yale Univ. Press, 1977).

See also nos. 149, 159.

3. Censuses of Quartos and Folios.

139. Bartlett, Henrietta C., and Alfred W. Pollard. *A Census of Shakespeare's Plays In Quarto, 1594–1709.* New Haven: Yale University Press, 1916. Revised and extended edition, New Haven: Yale Univ. Press; Oxford: Clarendon Press, 1939.

Bartlett and Pollard record all separate editions before 1709 of quartos of 19 plays: *Hamlet, 1 Henry IV, 2 Henry IV, Henry V, Caesar, Lear, Love's Labour's, Macbeth, Merchant, Merry Wives, Dream, Much Ado, Othello, Richard II, Richard III, Romeo, The Shrew, Titus,* and *Troilus*; they list each known copy of each edition and issue with its history since publication. They append a list of unidentified copies to which they have located references. The 1916 edition includes an introduction signed by both authors; it discusses the nature of the extant quartos in terms derived from Pollard's *Shakespeare's Folios and Quartos* (no. 183), and it provides some history of the establishment of great collections of quartos and their donation to public institutions. The 1939 edition (prepared by Bartlett alone) is an update of 1916 but without the introduction. Neither edition includes *Contention*, *True Tragedy*, and *Pericles;* Bartlett explains in the revised edition that in 1916 *Contention* and *True Tragedy* were not regarded as Shakespearean, and that in 1939 they are regarded merely as first drafts; she continues to omit *Pericles* because Lee had published a census of its copies in an edition.

140. Bartlett, Henrietta C. *Mr William Shakespeare: Original and Early Editions of his Quartos and Folios; His Source Books and Those Containing Contemporary Notices*. New Haven: Yale Univ. Press; Oxford: Oxford Univ. Press, 1923.

In a supplement to Bartlett and Pollard's *Census* (no. 139) Bartlett provides a listing with full bibliographic descriptions of editions in quarto, octavo, and folio printed before 1709 of both plays and poems. The book also contains similar lists for apocryphal works attributed to Shakespeare, for books which he "may have read or to which he refers" (xv), and for books containing allusions to Shakespeare.

141. Lee, Sidney. *A Supplement to the Reproduction in Facsimile of the First Folio Edition (1623) ... containing A Census of Extant Copies with some Account of their History and Condition*. Oxford: Clarendon Press, 1902.

In this supplement to his facsimile Lee produces the results of his attempt to locate and describe all extant copies of the First Folio. He records and gives the known history of 156 copies "in varying conditions of cleanliness and completeness" (7), classifying them according to four categories: perfect copies; imperfect copies; defective copies; and "copies otherwise unclassed owing to lack of full description." In the introduction he also presents a history of sales and prices; a discussion of the incidence of facsimile pages being used for repair of copies; a review of prior attempts at a census; and some observations on the difficulty of establishing copies' recension. In *Notes and Additions to the Census of Copies of the Shakespeare First Folio* (London: Oxford University Press, 1906, reprinted with revisions from *The Library*, n.s. 7 [1906], 113–39), Lee updates his work to 24 May 1906, corrects errors of description and attribution in his 1902 census, and adds information about 14 further copies that have come to his attention since its publication. See West's more recent census, no. 142.

142. West, Anthony James. "Provisional New Census of the Shakespeare First Folio." *The Library*, 6th series, 17 (1995): 60–73.

West presents an interim report on his census of copies of the First

Folio, aiming to provide information and to provoke further information from others. He accounts for all copies mentioned by Lee (no. 141); his list contains 228 numbered copies, including 13 unfound (copies Lee cited but which West has not found), but excluding those classed as untraced (copies that neither Lee nor West has located) or lost (a copy unknown to Lee, since lost). He lists the copies by three geographical regions: United Kingdom and Ireland; United States and Canada; the rest of the world.

B. Early Commentary and Editions before 1900.

143. Capell, Edward. Introduction to *Mr William Shakespeare his Comedies, Histories, and Tragedies*, 1: 1-74. 10 vols. London, 1767.

In his introduction (vol. 1) Capell states that he has consulted more quartos than anyone before him, 14 quartos whose texts he regards as reliable and 6 others that he regards as of inferior quality (including *Henry V*, *Merry Wives*, and Q1 *Romeo*, later designated as Bad Quartos). He analyzes the qualities of the quartos, criticizing their lack of act and scene divisions, their misassignment of speeches, and their imperfect lineation of verse; in examining the First Folio he recognizes that it printed quarto texts where available. He argues that the earliest text is the most reliable text, since each printing is based on the one before. He reviews the prior editions, and also defends *1 Henry VI*, *2 Henry VI*, *3 Henry VI*, *Love's Labour's*, *The Shrew*, and *Titus* as genuine Shakespearean plays. Capell explains his edition fully in the first two volumes of *Notes and Various Readings to Shakespeare* (3 vols.; London, 1779-83). He discusses problem passages in lengthy notes, correcting some of his earlier editorial decisions and proposing new emendations. He records readings and emendations adopted by previous editors, claiming thereby to present a comprehensive representation of the textual history of each play.

144. Clark, William George, John Glover, and William Aldis Wright, eds. *The Works of William Shakespeare*. 9 vols. Cambridge and London: Macmillan, 1863-66.

In their preface to vol. 1 Clark and Glover present their principles in preparing this edition. They argue for the primacy of the Folio text, although they know that its quality is variable; they are aware that many F texts were printed from quarto copy and posit that some may have been printed from transcripts; they accept quarto variants where there are "quartos of authority," and print all variants in notes or, if long, "*literatim* in a smaller type after the received text" (ix). They propose to disregard the punctuation of the earliest printings. In the preface to vol. 9 Clark and Wright review their editorial principles, stating that in cases where a quarto was printed before the Folio the quarto is the "best authority," and justifying their modernization of spelling and their caution in emendation. The prefaces to vols. 2–8 contain details of the textual history of each play and a summary of Clark and Wright's editorial decisions for plays existing in quarto and folio. This is the major scholarly edition of the nineteenth century, and its text provided the basis for the Globe edition, which became the standard text for reading and for the citation of line references into the early twentieth century.

145. Heminge, John, and Henry Condell. "To the great Variety of Readers." In William Shakespeare, *Comedies, Histories, and Tragedies*. London, 1623.

Heminge and Condell express regret that Shakespeare did not collect and publish his plays himself. They explain that they "haue collected and publish'd them; and so to haue publish'd them, as where (before) you were abus'd with diuerse stolne, and surreptitious copies, maimed, and deformed by the frauds and stealthes of iniurious impostors, that expos'd them: euen those, are now offer'd to your view cur'd, and perfect of their limbes; and all the rest, absolute in their numbers, as he conceiued the[m]." Moreover, they add that Shakespeare's "mind and hand went together: And what he thought, he vttered with that easinesse, that wee haue scarse receiued from him a blot in his papers" (A3r). See nos. 4, 136.

146. Jonson, Ben. *Timber, or Discoveries*. London, 1641. Repr. in *Ben Jonson*. Ed. C. H. Herford and Percy and Evelyn Simpson, 8: 555–649. 11 vols. Oxford: Clarendon Press, 1925–52.

Jonson records a memory that "the Players have often mentioned it as an honour to *Shakespeare*, that in his writing, (whatsoever he penn'd) hee never blotted out line. My answer hath beene, Would he had blotted a thousand" (647–50; 8: 583). He adds that Shakespeare had "brave notions, and gentle expressions: wherein hee flow'd with that facility, that sometime it was necessary he should be stop'd" (657–59; 8: 584). These passages have been used by some textual scholars as evidence of Shakespeare's writing habits and of the nature of his manuscript drafts.

147. Malone, Edmond. *The Plays and Poems of William Shakespeare*. 10 vols. London, 1790.

Malone is aware of fifteen plays in quarto before the Folio. Although he believes them stolen from the playhouses and printed surreptitiously, he regards them as "in general" of more authority than the Folio texts, which he regards as often printed from quarto copies rather than from new manuscripts. He regards the quartos of *Henry V* and *Merry Wives* as imperfect and declares Q1 *Romeo* an "imperfect sketch" (vol. 1, part 1, xviii). Unlike earlier editors he prints the poems as well, rejecting all editions subsequent to the first. He includes *Pericles* among the plays as containing Shakespeare's hand; he prints *Titus* separately in vol. 10 as a tragedy "erroneously ascribed" to Shakespeare (he is aware of the 1611 quarto of *Titus* but does not include it in the initial fifteen). Malone's edition is the major edition of the eighteenth century; through extensive archival research into the life and examination of the earliest printed evidence he endeavors to establish an "authentic" Shakespeare text independent of contemporary taste. See De Grazia (no. 210).

148. Rowe, Nicholas. *The Works of Mr William Shakespeare.* 6 vols. London, 1709.

Rowe bases his edition in six volumes on the Fourth Folio but does not reproduce the seven plays added in the Third Folio (no. 246). In dividing the plays into acts and scenes, regularizing the speech headings, and adding a list of dramatis personae for each play, he establishes the format in which the plays are customarily presented.

See also nos. 206, 223, 247.

C. General Studies.

149. Blayney, Peter W. M. *The First Folio of Shakespeare.* Washington, D.C.: Folger Shakespeare Library, 1991.

Published in conjunction with an exhibition, *The First Folio of Shakespeare*, at the Folger Shakespeare Library, this booklet contains an introduction to all the major issues concerning the Folio. Blayney discusses the origins of the work, its printer and publishers; he describes the history of the printing, including a description of the habits of compositors (with illustrations that demonstrate how compositors are identified) and an explanation of proof correction (with reproductions of examples from proof pages). He summarizes the negotiations for obtaining rights to the copy for the plays, with particular attention to *Troilus* and the peculiarities of its printing. He provides information about probable prices, known sales, and the cost of binding. He also presents a review of the variety of conditions in which copies survive with explanation of the practice of breaking up and making up copies.

150. Blayney, Peter W. M. *The Texts of "King Lear" and their Origins.* Vol. 1, *Nicholas Okes and the First Quarto.* Cambridge: Cambridge Univ. Press, 1982.

Blayney presents a comprehensive study of the printing of the First Quarto of *Lear*, which he places in December 1607 and January 1608. He describes at length the history and practices of Nicholas Okes's printing house, explaining each stage of the process and documenting fully the habits of compositors and the conduct of proofreading and stop-press correction. He proposes that the copy for Q1 *Lear* was probably foul papers but perhaps a transcript of them. The numerous appendixes contain lists of books printed by Okes between 1604 and 1609, details of his types and ornaments, and lists of press-variants in Okes's quartos of 1607 and 1608, including those in the Q1 of *Lear*. This is the most comprehensive study ever of the printing of a play text of this period; the discussions of composition and of proofreading and correction are particularly valuable introductions to those subjects.

151. Chambers, E. K. *William Shakespeare: A Study of Facts and Problems.* 2 vols. Oxford: Clarendon Press, 1930.

In vol. 1 Chambers proceeds from a summary of the facts of the life to a comprehensive introduction to the textual evidence of Shakespeare's works. He presents what is known about the written materials of the playhouse, including extant playbooks and manuscripts for private reading, and about stage censorship. He addresses the general issues of the practice of printing houses and the nature of printers' copy; he considers abridgment and adaptation as likely features of the life of a play, but rejects the disintegrationist dedication to multiple authorship. For the individual plays and poems, there is a detailed discussion of textual origins and characteristics: entries in the Stationers' Register, details of publication including bibliographical descriptions of title pages, and a summary of the current scholarship concerning the printing of the text. See no. 17.

152. Dessen, Alan, and Leslie Thomson. *A Dictionary of Stage Directions in English Drama, 1580–1642.* Cambridge: Cambridge Univ. Press, 1999.

Dessen and Thomson list over 900 terms that occur in stage directions of professional plays from 1580–1642; they propose that the data show that there was a common theatrical vocabulary during the period. For each entry (for instance, "coronet," "discover," "hair," "halberds," "rosemary," "study," "vanish") a definition is provided, followed by examples of how the term is used, additional instances of its occurrence, and cross-references to other entries. The dictionary derives from a database compiled by Thomson "of over 22,000 stage directions culled from roughly

TEXTUAL STUDIES   69

500 plays (some of them in more than one version)" (xi). For entries where the number of occurrences is not large, every instance is included; for more common terms representative examples are quoted and then further citations given. The dictionary ends with a list of terms by category (for instance, "actions," "body parts," "sounds and music," "special effects"), and a list of the plays and editions cited, compiled by Peter W. M. Blayney. See also Linda McJannet, *The Voice of Elizabethan Stage Directions: The Evolution of a Theatrical Code* (Newark: Univ. of Delaware Press, 1999), who discusses the historical evolution of stage directions, and their grammar, rhetoric, and distinctive vocabulary in texts of Shakespeare's time. See nos. 162, 163, 217.

153. Greg, W. W. *Collected Papers*, ed. J. C. Maxwell. Oxford: Clarendon Press, 1966.

Maxwell includes 30 of 37 articles that Greg had selected for publication prior to his death and adds three others. The book contains the following essays directly related to Shakespeare: "An Elizabethan Printer and His Copy"; "The Function of Bibliography in Literary Criticism illustrated in a study of the Text of *King Lear*"; "The Rationale of Copy-Text" (no. 215); "Time, Place, and Politics in *King Lear*"; "The Printing of Shakespeare's *Troilus and Cressida* in the First Folio"; "Shakespeare's Hand Once More" (see no. 267).

154. Greg, W. W. *Dramatic Documents From the Elizabethan Playhouses: Stage Plots: Actors' Parts: Prompt Books.* 2 vols. Oxford: Clarendon Press, 1931.

This compilation provides important documentary evidence for playhouse practice in Shakespeare's time. In vol. 1, "Reproductions and Transcripts," Greg presents in an oversize format photographic facsimiles and type transcriptions of the following: the six extant manuscript "plots" of plays of the period along with reprints of two others (a plot is an outline of the action of a play for use in the playhouse); the actor's "part" of Orlando from Greene's *Orlando Furioso*; and specimen pages from nine surviving "prompt books." Lists of actors mentioned in the plots and the parts they played are included in table form. In vol. 2, "Commentary," Greg discusses the general characteristics of each category of document and of the individual documents themselves; he concludes with a descriptive list of extant manuscript plays.

155. Greg, W. W. "On Certain False Dates in Shakespearian Quartos." *The Library*, 2nd series, 9 (1908): 113-31, 381-409.

Greg builds on the work of Alfred W. Pollard, who in "Shakespeare in the Remainder Market" (*Academy*, 2 June 1906, 528-29), identified four distinctive sets of quartos, one set bound in a single volume, among which were quartos printed by Thomas Pavier; recognizing their unusual uniformity of size but the various dates on the title pages, Pollard hypothesized that Thomas Pavier bought up "remainders" of some earlier editions of 1600 and 1608 which he then combined into single volumes with other plays that he was reprinting. However, from a study of several sets of Pavier quartos Greg notes that they display features that are unlikely to be associated with books printed at various earlier times, including a larger than usual page size, distinctive types, and a similarity of title page format with recurrent devices. His study of watermarks indicates conclusively that the whole set was printed at one time from one mixed stock of paper: Pavier was using up a quantity of remnants in 1619. He proposes that by falsifying the dates on the title pages Pavier was endeavoring to conceal that he was enjoined by the Lord Chamberlain from printing the plays. Subsequently, William Neidig, prompted by the work of Greg and Pollard, examines the title pages of the Pavier quartos and proves by measurement and photographic superimposition that areas of the various title pages are identical: for seven of the nine plays the printer used a single setting of type that he modified in each instance. On the basis of his observations Neidig is able to propose an order of printing of the Pavier quartos ("The Shakespeare Quartos of 1619," *Modern Philology*, 8 [1910]: 145-63).

156. Greg, W. W. *The Shakespeare First Folio: Its Bibliographical and Textual History.* Oxford: Clarendon Press, 1955.

Greg's study begins with a discussion of the origins of the printing of the Folio collection by William Jaggard for a publishing syndicate and of Jaggard's earlier printing of the Pavier quartos; he then discusses the nature of copyright in the period, the entry in the Stationers' Register of previously unpublished plays, and the prior printing history of previously printed plays. Three chapters on "Editorial Problems" follow. The first deals with the selection of plays for inclusion and the ordering in the collection and the nature of quarto texts; Greg accepts McKerrow's position that playtexts may have been printed from authorial drafts (see nos. 164, 165). The second deals with the copy at the disposal of compilers of the First Folio and describes the distinctive features of copy derived from foul papers and from promptbooks, specifically in relation to designation of characters in speech headings and to different forms of stage directions. In the third Greg discusses each play individually, describing the textual characteristics of any quarto printing and of the Folio text, and presenting a thesis concerning the origin of the copy for each. He concludes with a discussion of the process of the printing of the book, including the attribution of the composition to A and B and some discussion of the proofreading, but concluding with the observation that the study of the variants is at an early stage, but that evidence indicates that (*contra* Lee, no. 161) the printer was not careless in his work. Although some of Greg's views have been challenged, this remains a basic study of the Folio.

157. Hart, Alfred. "Acting Versions of Elizabethan Plays." *Review of English Studies* 10 (1934): 1–28.

Starting from his calculation that performance texts did not exceed 2,400 lines (see no. 158), Hart argues that abridgment of plays was customary; that all of Shakespeare's plays except *Errors*, *Two Gentlemen*, *Dream*, *Macbeth*, *Timon*, *Tempest*, and *Pericles* were abridged for performance; that Shakespeare neither revised his own plays nor rewrote those of others; that the first quartos of *Romeo*, *Henry V*, *Merry Wives*, and *Hamlet* were not first sketches, which he later expanded, but corrupt abridgments of acting versions; that of *Richard III*, *Richard II*, *2 Henry IV*, *Hamlet* (Q2), *Othello*, *Lear*, and *Troilus*, neither the quarto nor the Folio text is an acting version. Hart asserts that Shakespeare was "first and, above all, a poet and creative artist" (26) who, refusing to be bound by the constraints of the playhouse, wrote long plays in the knowledge that they would be abridged for performance, and that the play of 3,000 lines and more ceases to be written, even by Jonson, after 1616.

158. Hart, A. "The Length of Elizabethan and Jacobean Plays." *Review of English Studies* 8 (1932): 139–54.

Hart responds to commonplace assumptions that the average length of an Elizabethan play (estimated from calculations relating to Shakespearean texts) was about 3,000 lines, and that it was to such a length of play that audiences were accustomed; he objects to the invocation of such a norm in judgments concerning the relation of printed texts to performance. From a survey of 233 plays of the period 1564–1616 he concludes that few plays of 3,000 lines and upward were written, except by Shakespeare and Jonson; that Shakespeare's plays average about 2,750 lines in length, the English history plays being conspicuously long; that Jonson's plays were abnormally long for the period; and that the average length of all plays except Jonson's was about 2,500 lines. He explains the basis of his calculations in "The Number of Lines in Shakespeare's Plays," *Review of English Studies* 8 (1932): 19–28. See also his essay, "The Time Allotted for Representation of Elizabethan and Jacobean Plays," *Review of English Studies* 8 (1932): 395–413, in which he relates these judgments to references in at least a dozen texts of the period to two hours as the length of performance in the Elizabethan playhouse.

159. Hinman, Charlton. *The Printing and Proof-Reading of the First Folio of Shakespeare.* 2 vols. Oxford: Clarendon Press, 1963.

Hinman's extensive study presents a reconstruction of all aspects of the process of the printing of the First Folio. Hinman initially surveys the books Jaggard was printing in 1621–23, discusses the copyrights of the plays, gives a bibliographical description of the book, and estimates the print run at about 1,200 copies; he pays little attention to questions concerning printers' copy. He then describes the kinds of physical evidence for the printing process and their uses in his reconstruction: the identification of individual types, of box rules, headlines, and running titles. He discusses the distinctive characteristics that identify five compositors. Proposing that Isaac Jaggard was the proofreader, he argues that there is no evidence of systematic proofreading, which was occasional and did not necessarily involve reference to copy; he lists and discusses fully each identified proof correction. After presenting at the end of vol. 1 a chronology of the printing, which he states began in either late 1621 or early 1622, he devotes vol. 2 to a detailed analysis of the printing process. McKenzie (no. 221) and Blayney (nos. 136, 149) challenge Hinman's conception of proofreading; Blayney challenges the size of the print run and some aspects of Hinman's identification of the compositors in nos. 136, 149.

160. Jackson, MacD. P. "The transmission of Shakespeare's text." In *The Cambridge Companion to Shakespeare*, ed. Stanley Wells, 163–85. Cambridge: Cambridge Univ. Press, 1986.

Jackson presents a concise introduction to major issues concerning the text. Starting from questions of the identification of the plays that Shakespeare wrote, of collaborative writing and the constitution of the canon, he discusses the concepts of foul papers and prompt copy in relation to quarto and Folio texts, and describes Bad Quartos as memorially reconstructed texts. He examines specimen quarto and Folio variants and their implications for editing, and he considers the possibility of revision. He explains the practice of casting off copy and setting by formes, the nature of stop-press correction, and the identification of compositors. He illustrates his argument with numerous examples.

161. Lee, Sidney, ed. Introduction to *Shakespeares Comedies, Histories and Tragedies, Being a Reproduction in Facsimile ... with Introduction and Census of Copies*, xi–xxxv. Oxford: Clarendon Press, 1902.

Lee discusses the origins of the printed texts of Shakespeare's plays. He states that publishers of quartos exercised their right to print through obtaining a licence from the Stationers' Company, ignoring authors' wishes; that printers were careless of the quality of their copy, often gaining it from shorthand or longhand reports; and that most quartos were printed from imperfect playhouse transcripts of no authority. He proposes that authorial original drafts had already been treated with disrespect in the playhouse: theatrical managers excised scenes and passages before the playhouse scrivener made up the "prompt-copy," in which other revisions were made. Lee argues that the copy for the First Folio was of three kinds: "prompt-copies," of which he presumes a large number of originals burned in the 1613 fire at the Globe playhouse; quartos; and private transcripts. He suggests that the relative absence in the Folio texts of stage directions, act and scene divisions, and lists of dramatis personae indicate the primacy of private transcripts. He proposes that the arrangement of the plays within the three classifications is random. Lee discusses the nature of the paper and the types and ornaments, the states of the portrait, and the order of the printing of the plays; he argues from misprints and inconsistencies of spelling that the printing of the plays was inadequately supervised. He concludes with a brief survey of the Second, Third, and Fourth Folios. Lee writes here as a figure of authority at the turn of the century; Pollard's challenge and rejection of Lee's thinking about playhouse behavior, the nature of printers' copy, and the printing process initiate in 1909 the New Bibliography (see no. 183). See also no. 141.

162. Long, William B. "'A bed / for woodstock': A Warning for the Unwary." *Medieval and Renaissance Drama in England* 2 (1985): 91–118.

In an examination of the characteristics of surviving manuscript playbooks that is primarily devoted to that of *Woodstock*, Long argues that the presumptions about the nature and features of playbooks advanced by Chambers (no. 151) and Greg (no. 156) and adopted as fact by generations of editors are unfounded. Long shows that no conventional regular pattern of preparation or consistent terminology can be generalized from the evidence, that not all marginalia relate directly to the stage action, and that the variety of the entries must be interpreted sensitively to discern particular significance. He insists that the companies operated successfully with playbooks that do not conform to modern expectations. See nos. 152, 163, 217.

163. Long, William B. "Stage-Directions: A Misinterpreted Factor in Determining Textual Provenance." *TEXT* 2 (1985): 121–37.

Long argues from an examination of extant playbooks that it is not possible to distinguish stage directions written by an author from those added in the playhouse on the basis of syntactic form or distinctive content; he states that they do not conform to the modes that Chambers (no. 151) and Greg (no. 156) have assumed to be identifiable. He demonstrates that to achieve the regularity of form and specificity of detail that Greg's theories assume to have been characteristic of playbooks, it would have been necessary for many stage directions written in authors' hands in surviving playbooks to have been altered by a bookholder or playhouse official. See also nos. 152, 162, 217.

164. McKerrow, R. B. "The Elizabethan Printer and Dramatic Manuscripts." *The Library*, 4th series, 12 (1931–32): 253–75. Repr. in *Ronald Brunlees McKerrow: A Selection of His Essays*. Compiled by John Phillip Immroth. Metuchen, N.J.: Scarecrow Press, 1974.

McKerrow observes that the printing of plays was inferior to that of other books and suggests that the copy provided to the printer was not a fair copy but an authorial draft from which a fair copy had been made to serve as promptbook in the playhouse. He argues that no company would have been ready to allow the promptbook to leave the playhouse to be used in the printing shop, and that no fresh copy would have been submitted for licensing for publication. Moreover, he establishes four distinguishing features of promptbooks that would be expected to be apparent in a play printed from one: warnings for actors' entrances or for properties; properties needed by an actor after entrance; actors' names appearing as glosses on the name of the character, not as a speech heading; and the early marking of characters' entrances. With McKerrow 1935 (no. 165) this article influenced subsequent thinking about the identification of printers' copy. For a challenge to McKerrow's arguments see Long (nos. 162, 163) and articles in Williams (no. 241).

165. McKerrow, R. B. "A Suggestion Regarding Shakespeare's Manuscripts." *Review of English Studies* 11 (1935): 459–65. Repr. in Williams (no. 241).

Observing that in some printed texts the designations of speakers' names is consistent whereas in others they are irregular, McKerrow advances the hypothesis that irregular designation indicates that a play was printed from an authorial manuscript, and that consistency of designation is a mark of origin from "some sort of fair copy, perhaps made by a professional scribe" (464). Editors would therefore expect to find different kinds of errors appearing in these two categories of texts. This highly influential article is challenged in several articles in Williams (no. 241).

166. Taylor, Gary, and John Jowett. *Shakespeare Reshaped 1606–1623.* Oxford: Clarendon Press, 1993.

Three separate studies by Taylor and Jowett discuss the evidence for the modification of play texts after initial composition. In "The Structure of Performance: Act-Intervals in the London Theatres, 1576–1642" (3–50), Taylor demonstrates that in the context of reports of performances, changes in the formats of manuscript and printed texts indicate that a musical interval between acts, a custom of private playhouses, became the custom of public playhouses between 1607 and 1616; he states that the textual evidence suggests that the practice was universal after 1615. Taylor also examines the phenomenon in F of the apparently inconsistent expurgation from the texts of oaths and profanities (" 'Swounds Revisited: Theatrical, Editorial, and Literary Expurgation," 51–106). He argues that expurgation almost always derives from the playhouse, and that one should not assume that scribes, publishers, or printers expurgated texts. Jowett and Taylor propose in an extensive study (" 'With New Additions': Theatrical Interpolation in *Measure for Measure*," 107–236) that the Shakespeare texts contain passages by hands other than the author; they argue that two passages from *Measure* are unShakespearean interpolations added around 1621, and that Middleton was the author of some of the new material. In a "Postscript" (237–43) Taylor discusses some implications of these studies for editorial practice and asserts specifically that "the bulk of Shakespeare's oeuvre comes down to us in editions which reflect non-authorial literary transcripts" (243) rather than authorial or playhouse documents, a position which, he notes, was maintained by Lee (see no. 161) before the ascendance of the New Bibliography.

167. Walker, Alice. *Textual Problems of the First Folio.* Cambridge: Cambridge Univ. Press, 1953.

Walker discusses the origins of the Folio texts of *Richard III*, *Lear*, *Troilus*, *2 Henry IV*, *Hamlet*, and *Othello*. She argues that in each case the printer's copy was a quarto that had been corrected by collation with a manuscript, either foul papers, transcript, or promptbook, and that each text presents different challenges to the editor, particularly in the light of the varied origins of the quarto texts and of the habits of Compositors A and B.

168. Walton, J. K. *The Quarto Copy for the First Folio of Shakespeare.* Dublin: Dublin Univ. Press, 1971.

Walton conducts an extensive enquiry to discern the nature of the copy behind those F texts that had previously been published in quarto. For each play he ascertains which quarto provided the copy, whether the quarto was altered as a result of comparison with either a promptbook or foul papers, and that in the case of *2 Henry IV*, *Hamlet*, and *Othello* the copy for the F text was a manuscript and not a quarto.

169. Wells, Stanley, and Gary Taylor, with John Jowett and William Montgomery. *William Shakespeare: A Textual Companion*. Oxford: Clarendon Press, 1987. Repr., with corrections, New York: W. W. Norton, 1997.

This companion volume to the Oxford *Complete Works* (1986) initially and to the *Norton Shakespeare* (1997) (no. 3) subsequently contains a series of studies by the Oxford editors. In the "General Introduction" (1–68) Gary Taylor discusses the principles and practice of editing, the conception of foul papers and promptbooks, censorship, revision, private transcripts, and memorial reconstruction; he summarizes the printing process, reviews the history of the editing of Shakespeare, and examines the nature of emendation. In "The Canon and Chronology of Shakespeare's Texts" (69–144) Taylor reviews the external evidence for both and describes and illustrates the techniques of using internal evidence; there is a brief individual summary of the status of each play, followed by a similar treatment of apocryphal plays and poems that are not included in either edition (see no. 250). After a "Summary of Control-Texts," the list of "Attributions to Compositors of the First Folio," and a description of "Editorial Procedures" a full study is presented of the text of each play, written by the editor who assumed primary responsibility for the text in the edition; the collations are very full and the notes extensive.

170. Wilson, F. P. *Shakespeare and the New Bibliography*. Rev. and ed. Helen Gardner. Oxford: Clarendon Press, 1970.

This book is a revised version of an essay entitled "Shakespeare and the 'New Bibliography'," originally published in *The Bibliographical Society, 1892–1942: Studies In Retrospect* (ed. Frank C. Francis. London: Oxford Univ. Press for the Bibliographical Society, 1945, 76–135). The introduction by Helen Gardner describes the origins of the essay and of its revision; the footnotes contain Wilson's own updatings made in 1948 in anticipation of republication and those of Helen Gardner made for the 1970 revision. Wilson presents initially a brief history of textual thought before 1909, the beginning of the New Bibliography, and then a series of chapters on the publication of plays, their printing, and the nature of dramatic manuscripts. In a discussion of the discrimination of the copy for the quartos and the Folio, he expresses doubts about Greg's distinction between literary and theatrical stage directions and about the significance of actors' names as speech headings; he explains the concept of the

TEXTUAL STUDIES 77

memorial origins of Bad Quartos while remaining skeptical of the role of shorthand in their composition; he regards the quarto texts of *Richard III* and *Lear* as reported versions of acted plays. He concludes with a brief history of editing from Malone to Greg. At all times Wilson presents the history of particular modes of thought. This study is a good summary of the principles of the New Bibliography.

See also nos. 57, 133, 136, 137.

D. Quartos Good and Bad.

171. Bracy, William. *The Merry Wives of Windsor: The History and Transmission of Shakespeare's Text.* Univ. of Missouri Studies 25, no. 1. Columbia: Univ. of Missouri Press, 1952.

In an initial general study of Bad Quartos, Bracy rejects the "first-sketch" and shorthand theories, and then argues that memorial reconstruction is an inadequate explanation of the phenomena of the texts. In an examination of Q *Merry Wives* he argues that it is a "version legitimately and drastically abridged and adapted to special conditions of performance" (104); the abridgment was made by an official "adapter-reviser," probably for a touring company smaller than the London company, and may have undergone further "debasement" at the actors' hands.

172. Burkhart, Robert E. *Shakespeare's Bad Quartos: Deliberate Abridgements Designed for Performance By a Reduced Cast.* The Hague, Holland: Mouton, 1975.

Burkhart rejects memorial reconstruction as an unsatisfactory hypothesis for the origin of Bad Quartos. He proposes instead that they are versions of the Good texts which have been shortened to facilitate performance by casts of actors smaller than those required by the Good versions, and that the texts are not so corrupt as proponents of reporting suggest. The shorter version of a play was created by an official "author-adapter" for the company.

173. Cloud, Random (McLeod, Randall). "The Marriage of the Good and Bad Quartos." *Shakespeare Quarterly* 33 (1982): 421-31.

Random Cloud begins by arguing that the terminology of Good and Bad in relation to quartos prejudices the thinking of critics and editors and thereby conduces to the suppression of important evidence concerning the nature and variety of Shakespeare's writing; he argues that Good and Bad are matters of taste and not appropriate terms for the discussion of literary works. He focuses his discussion on examples from the 1980

Arden edition of *Romeo*, showing how the constraints of the editorial format deny the richness of Shakespeare's writing; he proposes that in cases where plays survive in multiple texts, the conventional modernized edition is a wish-fulfillment.

174. Craig, Hardin. *A New Look at Shakespeare's Quartos*. Stanford: Stanford Univ. Press, 1961.

Craig takes issue with the discrimination of quartos into Bad and Good, attacking previous scholars such as Pollard for using an inadequate methodology. He rejects the theory of memorial reconstruction and argues for various explanations for the states of different texts. He emphasizes the constant adjustments and modifications to which play manuscripts were subject, arguing that some quartos result from acts of abridgment and asserting that variation is a product of alterations made during the life of the play in the playhouse.

175. Davidson, Adele. "'Some by Stenography?' Stationers, Shorthand, and the Early Shakespearean Quartos." *Publications of the Bibliographical Society of America* 90 (1996): 417–49.

Davidson argues for a reassessment of the role of shorthand in the publication of playtexts. She states that shorthand systems were a more prominent feature of the literary culture than has been supposed, in that they were used for rapid copying from manuscripts as well as for taking down speech. Davidson relates the publication of works on shorthand to the printers of some Shakespeare plays. In an examination of the variants between Q and F *Lear* she indicates that many anomalies in the Q text can be explained as the consequence of the reconstruction of shorthand notation, specifically to the system of John Willis known as stenography, and proposes a reconsideration of the concept of revision in relation to *Lear* in the light of the possibility that a manuscript was copied with the aid of stenography.

176. Duthie, George Ian. *Elizabethan Shorthand and the First Quarto of "King Lear."* Oxford: Basil Blackwell, 1949.

Duthie examines the systems of shorthand in operation in 1608; he concludes that the systems were not capable of producing in the playhouse a stenographic transcription of a play of such quality that it could have provided the printer's copy for Q1 *Lear*. See no. 175.

177. Greg, W. W., ed. Introduction to *Shakespeare's Merry Wives of Windsor 1602*, vii–lvi. Oxford: Clarendon Press, 1910.

Greg examines the 1602 quarto of *Merry Wives* in the light of Pollard's categorization of Bad Quartos (see no. 183). In the process of explaining the divergences between the quarto and Folio texts of *Merry Wives* Greg posits the roles of three figures other than the author who influenced the Q text of the play: first, a reporter, who provided the copy for the printer of the quarto ("Busby's wretched piracy," xliii); second, an adapter, who at an early stage of the play's existence cut and rewrote parts of the author's text; and third, a reviser, who at some point amplified and rewrote this acting text. On the basis of his perception of the unusual accuracy of the part of the Host amid the corruptions elsewhere in Q he advances the view that the quarto text was produced from memory by the actor who played the part of the Host, perhaps dictating to another, perhaps in collaboration with a reporter (xli), perhaps alone (xliii). Greg conceives a speculative narrative of the textual history of the play, concluding with regret that the play "as Shakespeare wrote it" cannot be recovered (xlii–xliv). In this essay Greg introduces the idea of the role of memorial reconstruction by an actor in relation to the Bad Quartos.

178. Greg, W. W. *Two Elizabethan Stage Abridgments: The Battle of Alcazar and Orlando Furioso.* The Malone Society Extra Volume 1922. Oxford: Oxford University Press, 1922.

Following the work on Bad Quartos of Pollard (no. 183) and John Dover Wilson and his own study of the quarto of *Merry Wives* (no. 177), Greg examines two other plays of the 1590s in order to establish the existence of "a class of shortened texts of Elizabethan plays in general" (1) not limited to the works of Shakespeare. From an examination of the quarto of Peele's *The Battle of Alcazar* in comparison with the extant "plot" of the play (a plot is an outline of the action of a play for use in the playhouse), Greg concludes that the quarto "represents a shortened and simplified version of the play" (45), designed for performance by a small cast; he reprints the whole of the "plot." His comparison of the text of the quarto of Greene's *Orlando Furioso* with the surviving "part" of Orlando that belonged to Edward Alleyn leads him to conclude that the quarto represents a memorial reconstruction of the play by a touring company that lacked a prompt copy and that had already modified the play considerably; he reprints the part and the relevant passages from the quarto in parallel.

179. Hart, Alfred. *Stolne and Surreptitious Copies: A Comparative Study of Shakespeare's Bad Quartos.* Melbourne: Melbourne Univ. Press, 1942.

From an extensive review of comparative evidence from Bad Quartos and their Good textual counterparts, including examinations of vocabulary, use of rare words, verse structure, rhyme, and repetitions, Hart argues for the acceptance of the theory of memorial reconstruction in relation to *Contention, True Tragedy, Hamlet, Henry V, Romeo,* and *Merry Wives*: "the text of a bad quarto rests on the oral transmission of what an actor could recollect of a part written out by a scribe from the acting version made officially from the author's manuscript" (444). He asserts that the "authentic text" derived from the author's manuscript or a transcript of it.

180. Irace, Kathleen O. *Reforming the "Bad" Quartos: Performance and Provenance of Six Shakespearean First Editions.* Newark: Univ. of Delaware Press, 1994.

Irace examines the Bad Quartos, which she calls "short quartos," anew. In part 1 she surveys their distinctive "performance features," reviewing the variations in plot, characterization, and stage business between them and their comparable Good texts; she draws significantly upon performance history for illustrations of their playing potential and concludes that as texts they are related to performance. In part 2 she first rejects the possibility that they may represent early drafts of the longer texts, and then proceeds to a computer-assisted re-examination of the evidence for memorial reconstruction. She concludes that they do derive from acts of memorial reconstruction; she identifies the probable reporters, providing charts of her findings in a series of appendixes. She argues that all the short quartos underwent adaptation in the process of reconstruction, but she suggests that *Contention* and Q1 *Romeo* may have been based on intermediate abridgments.

181. Maguire, Laurie E. *Shakespeare's Suspect Texts.* Cambridge: Cambridge Univ. Press, 1996.

Maguire studies the Shakespearean Bad Quartos, which she renames "suspect texts," in the context of a reassessment of the concept of memorial reconstruction and of a survey of all the texts of the period that have been identified as memorially reconstructed. In part 1 she traces the development of the New Bibliography and locates and judges Greg's career within it; she describes his articulation of the theory of memorial reconstruction (see nos. 177, 178) and its subsequent application by others. Next Maguire considers the historical evidence concerning the reporting of speeches, sermons, and plays in the period and in the eighteenth century, and then examines examples of memory, including the memories of actors in the BBC Shakespeare series, which provide classifiable instances of the kinds of errors that those actors made. In part 2 she establishes from a review of all the traits that scholars have identified as marks of memorial reconstruction those that she believes can be reliable indicators.

Employing these indicators, she reviews forty-one texts, including those of Shakespeare that scholars have discerned as memorially reconstructed, presenting a summary of her conclusions on each in tabular form. Of the Shakespeare plays she considers that Q1 *Merry Wives* is probably a memorial reconstruction; that Q1 *Hamlet* and *Pericles* may possibly be; and that *A Shrew* is also probably memorially reconstructed.

182. McMillin, Scott. "Casting for Pembroke's Men: The *Henry VI* Quartos and *The Taming of A Shrew*." *Shakespeare Quarterly* 23 (1972): 141–59. Repr. in Orgel and Keilen (no. 238).

Accepting the hypothesis that *Contention* and *True Tragedy* are derivatives of 2 *Henry VI* and 3 *Henry VI*, McMillin argues that distinctive features of those reduced texts are the consequence of an abridgment for a company of eleven actors and four boys rather than the thirteen actors and four boys needed to perform the F texts; on the basis of the curtailment of the leading boy's role and the elimination of the more elaborate poetry of the F texts, he suggests that the smaller company may have been composed of less experienced performers. He identifies a number of the players by name and finds them associated with the text of *A Shrew*.

183. Pollard, Alfred W. *Shakespeare's Folios and Quartos: A Study in the Bibliography of Shakespeare's Plays, 1594–1685*. London: Methuen, 1909.

In the course of responding to Lee's rejection of the quarto texts as "stolne and surreptitious copies" (see Lee, no. 161, and Heminge and Condell, no. 145) Pollard presents a full bibliographical study of the quartos and folios with numerous illustrations. In the light of his description of printing house practices he argues that the texts of the majority of the quartos are Good, deriving from authorial or authorized playhouse sources. However, he also discriminates a category of "piratical" Bad Quartos, which includes *Romeo* 1597, *Henry V* 1600, *Merry Wives* 1602, *Hamlet* 1603, and *Pericles* 1609, whose origins are unclear but certainly not authorial, and which derive in some cases from reporters sent to performances to take down the play by shorthand: these are the "stolne and surreptitious copies." He presents a narrative of the identification of the Pavier quartos of 1619 (see no. 155), reviews evidence from types and devices and also from Greg's work on watermarks, argues that these quartos constitute a special class, and speculates on the motives behind the false dates on the title pages. He documents the printing of the First Folio, discussing the partners in the venture, the holders of copyright for individual plays, the ordering of the plays in the volume, their editing, and the printing process in Jaggard's printing house. He concludes with bibliographical descriptions and discussion of post-1623 quartos, including those of plays added in the Third Folio, and of the Second, Third, and Fourth Folios. Pollard's study rejected the work of Lee (see no. 161), and with its invention of the categories of Good and Bad Quartos his study became the foundation of the New Bibliography. He developed his argument further in *Shakespeare's Fight with the Pirates and the Problems of the Transmission of His Text* (London: A. Moring, 1917. 2nd edition, rev. with an introduction, Cambridge: Cambridge Univ. Press, 1920). Pollard's classification of Bad Quartos has been debated widely (see this section, passim); Blayney argues against their origins in piracy or unauthorized publication (see Blayney in Cox and Kastan, no. 233).

184. Urkowitz, Steven. "Good News about Bad Quartos." In *Bad Shakespeare: Revaluations of the Shakespeare Canon*, ed. Maurice Charney, 189–206. Rutherford, N.J.: Fairleigh Dickinson Univ. Press, 1988.

Urkowitz re-examines the modes of argument and rhetoric that construct the categories of Good and Bad Quartos, attending particularly to the writings of W. W. Greg, Peter Alexander, Alfred Hart, and Harold Jenkins. Rejecting the concept of memorial reconstruction, he argues that the variants between Bad and Good texts of plays should be treated as differences related to stages in composition rather than as evidence of deterioration or corruption, and illustrates his position with examples from *2 Henry VI* and *Hamlet*. See also Steven Urkowitz, "Five Women Eleven Ways: Changing Images of Shakespeare's Characters in the Earliest Texts," in *Images of Shakespeare*, ed. Werner Habicht, D. J. Palmer, and Roger Pringle, 292–304 (Newark: Univ. of Delaware Press, 1988).

185. Werstine, Paul. "A Century of 'Bad' Quartos," *Shakespeare Quarterly* 50 (1999): 310–33.

Werstine describes the origin of the Bad Quarto hypothesis (Pollard, no. 183) and its association with the "memorial reconstruction" hypothesis (Greg, no. 177). After criticizing Greg's arguments concerning *Merry Wives*, he examines the evidence for the identification of the alleged reporters of *Merry Wives*, *Hamlet*, *Henry V*, and *Romeo*; acknowledging the potential persuasiveness of some elements, he demonstrates the inadequacy of the hypothesis to produce consistent explanations of the textual phenomena of each play. Maintaining that arguments that presume that Bad Quartos are the result of memorial reconstruction are characterized by circular reasoning, he challenges the notion that they are necessarily performance texts. Werstine notes that these texts may derive from memorial reconstruction, but asserts that the case is in no way proved.

186. Werstine, Paul. "Narratives about Printed Shakespearean Texts: 'Foul Papers' and 'Bad Quartos'." *Shakespeare Quarterly* 41 (1990): 65-86.

Werstine argues that the binarism that divides the quartos into two categories, Good and Bad, is a distinctive narrative structure developed by critics and scholars that has no foundation in evidence. He describes the history of the employment of the terms "foul papers" (authorial) and "memorial reconstruction" (by an actor or actors) as explanations for the origin of each kind of quarto, and asserts that there is no evidence for the existence of either; he regards the terms as products of the scholarly desire for individual agents as sources to explain complex phenomena in simple terms. He proposes that instead scholars should be aware of other possible narratives of origin, including that plays were, in Thomas Heywood's phrase, "coppied ... by ... eare," possibly not by actors, that authors sold plays directly to publishers, and that actors provided personal friends with copies of playhouse manuscripts, from whose text scenes had already been cut.

See also nos. 57, 133, 135, 136, 137, 139, 160, 211, 218, 219, 237a.

E. Revision.

187. Chambers, E. K. "The Disintegration of Shakespeare." *Proceedings of the British Academy* 11 (1924-25): 89-108. Published separately, London: Oxford Univ. Press, 1924.

In the British Academy Annual Shakespeare lecture of 1924 Chambers argues for the authorial integrity of the Shakespeare canon in the face of suggestions that some plays are revisions of others' work and that many contain additions by others' hands. After tracing an early history of textual disintegration and noting its impressionistic foundations, he rejects the theories of F. G. Fleay and J. M. Robertson that identify the writing of other playwrights in the texts. In rejecting the more recent "parallel speculations" of Pollard and Dover Wilson, which are based on textual bibliography, Chambers attacks the "doctrine of continuous copy"—that the playhouse "book of the play" was subject to intermittent abridgment, expansion, and revision by nonauthorial hands—and argues that the amount of revision in the Shakespeare canon is small. He adduces in support of this position the fact that "substantial revision" (17) would require resubmission for licensing to the Master of the Revels; he draws attention to the small amount of revision of the works of other playwrights apparent from the records in *Henslowe's Diary*. This study was influential in discouraging the consideration of revision in Shakespeare's plays for over forty years after its publication.

188. Coghill, Nevill. *Shakespeare's Professional Skills.* Cambridge: Cambridge Univ. Press, 1964.

Coghill argues that in two plays textual variation between the quarto and Folio texts of plays can be explained by postperformance revision. In chapter 4, "A Prologue and an 'Epilogue'" (78–97) he proposes that differences between Q and F *Troilus* derive from additions and alterations made between its initial performances at the Globe in 1602/3 and a revival for performance at one of the Inns of Court for Christmas 1608. In chapter 7, "Revision after Performance" (164–202), he performs a dramaturgical analysis of variant passages in Q and F *Othello* to conclude that each text represents a different stage in the performance history of the play. He argues that the F text is the product of a revision by Shakespeare some time after its first presentation, certainly after the passing of the Statute against Abuses of 1606.

189. Goldberg, Jonathan. "Textual Properties." *Shakespeare Quarterly* 37 (1986): 213–17.

Proposing that there is common ground between recent developments in textual criticism and poststructuralism, Goldberg argues that the discrimination of two versions of *Lear* is only the superficial treatment of a larger issue, the inevitable absence of an identifiable authorial text of any work. He stresses that "the Shakespearean text is a historical phenomenon" (215), a composite of the various processes that have influenced it in its composition, modification, and transmission, that there is no "original" to be established, and that in consequence there cannot be a "proper" or stable Shakespearean text.

190. Honigmann, E. A. J. "Shakespeare's Revised Plays: *King Lear* and *Othello*." *The Library*, 6th series, 4 (1982): 142–73.

Honigmann examines the issue of authorial revision in *Lear* and endorses the positions held by Taylor, Urkowitz, and Warren (see no. 197), although stating that not all variants between the texts should be attributed to revision by Shakespeare, since scribal and compositor error are always likely. He then argues, following Coghill (no. 188), that strategies of revision similar to those in *Lear* are discernible between Q and F *Othello*, and he attributes them to Shakespeare's hand. See also E. A. J. Honigmann, "Shakespeare as a Reviser" in *Textual Criticism and Literary Interpretation*, ed. Jerome J. McGann, 1–22 (Chicago: Univ. of Chicago Press, 1985). However, Honigmann alters his views on revision in *Othello* very substantially in *The Texts of "Othello" and Shakespearian Revision* (London: Routledge, 1996), disowning his earlier identification of strategies of revision, and suggesting that more attention should be given to corruption within it and *Lear*.

191. Honigmann, E. A. J. *The Stability of Shakespeare's Text*. London: Edward Arnold, 1965.

Distancing himself from the disintegrationist tradition in textual scholarship that considers many Shakespearean texts as revisions of others' work and assigns various parts of texts to various authors (see the discussion in Chambers, no. 187), Honigmann argues that variants between texts of plays existing in more than one state may be not symptoms of corruption but evidence of "first thoughts" and "second thoughts" of the author produced in the process of writing and copying before the play was delivered to the actors. He asserts that Shakespeare's habit of making changes both substantive and indifferent in the process of composition, a consequence of his fertility of invention rather than any desire for improvement, renders the texts of some plays (*Troilus, Othello, Lear*, for instance) unstable. He concludes that the editor will be obliged to recognize that reason will frequently afford little guidance in a situation where eclecticism is inevitable.

192. Ioppolo, Grace. *Revising Shakespeare*. Cambridge: Harvard University Press, 1991.

Ioppolo argues that Shakespeare, like other dramatists of his time, regularly revised his work. After a review of the current state of debate on revision, she presents the history of the idea of authorial revision in Shakespeare's work and then demonstrates the evidence for it in the work of Marston, Bale, Jonson, and Middleton. Starting with the duplicated passages in *Love's Labour's* and *Romeo* as examples of the survival in individual printed texts of Shakespeare's activity, she then discusses a number of plays that show evidence of authorial revision, concentrating notably on substantive variation between Q and F *Hamlet, Troilus*, and *Othello*. She devotes a final chapter to *Lear*, examining in detail the evidence for revision of the part of Cordelia.

193. Nosworthy, J. M. *Shakespeare's Occasional Plays: Their Origin and Transmission*. London: Edward Arnold, 1965.

Nosworthy considers four plays—*Macbeth, Troilus, Merry Wives*, and *Hamlet*—which he classifies as "occasional plays" since he posits that they were, "in the first place, designed for presentation before particular audiences on particular occasions" (1). In each case he distinguishes stages in the development of the play (in three of the four cases from variant states in quarto[s] and Folio) and discerns Shakespeare as the reviser of his own work. He posits that the evidence of these plays indicates that for the Folio, Heminge and Condell provided Jaggard with the "fullest available versions" (223) and the most accurate copy that they knew.

194. Taylor, Gary, and Michael Warren, eds. *The Division of the Kingdoms: Shakespeare's Two Versions of King Lear*. Oxford: Clarendon Press, 1983.

Following on the studies by Taylor, Urkowitz, and Warren (see no. 197), this collection of 12 essays by 11 authors (Thomas Clayton, Beth Goldring, MacD. P. Jackson, John Kerrigan, Randall McLeod, Gary Taylor, Steven Urkowitz, Michael Warren, Roger Warren, Stanley Wells, and Paul Werstine) challenges the conventional justification of a text of *Lear* derived by conflation of Q and F, arguing for the distinct nature of the Q and F texts. The studies are various, ranging from dramatic interpretation to historical study to technical bibliography. The majority of the essays explicitly support the idea of authorial revision as the source of the variation between the two texts. See also nos. 189, 190, 196.

195. Taylor, Gary. "Revising Shakespeare." *TEXT* 3 (1987): 285-304.

Through a series of linked studies Taylor argues for the acceptance of revision as a characteristic Shakespearean practice. He discusses initially passages in Q *Love's Labour's*, *Romeo* Q2, and *Hamlet* Q2 that scholars have traditionally accepted as evincing revision in the process of composition, and then passages in *Dream* and other plays that have been accepted as examples of revision at a later stage than initial composition. Acknowledging that absolute proof of revision after composition is not available, he argues that distinctive features of variant printed states of six plays—*2 Henry IV*, *Hamlet*, *Othello*, *Richard II*, *Troilus*, and *Lear*—and of certain sonnets constitutes a body of evidence that cannot be easily explained on any other basis. He concludes with a demonstration of the problems inherent in arguing that Shakespeare did not revise, including the necessity of assuming that he was abnormal in not engaging in a practice common among writers of his time and since.

196. Trousdale, Marion. "A Trip Through the Divided Kingdoms." *Shakespeare Quarterly* 37 (1986): 218-23.

Trousdale states that although she accepts that there are indeed two material and different texts of *Lear* the arguments of the revisionists do not establish satisfactorily the grounds for the differentiation. Specifically examining essays by Michael Warren and Gary Taylor (see no. 197) she challenges the formalist bias of their work, arguing that their interpretative methods do not preclude equally satisfactory interpretations that could lead to other conclusions, and are too dependent on the concept of the author for their validation.

197. Warren, Michael J. "Quarto and Folio *King Lear* and the Interpretation of Albany and Edgar." In *Shakespeare: Pattern of Excelling Nature*, ed. David Bevington and Jay L. Halio, 95–107. Newark: Univ. of Delaware Press, 1978.

Rejecting Chambers's arguments for the restriction of revision (no. 187) and basing his conclusions primarily on the variant interpretive potentials of the roles of Albany and Edgar and their consequences for dramatic structure, Warren argues that the quarto and Folio texts of *Lear* are separate authoritative versions of the play, F a revision of Q, and not two corrupt forms of a lost original; he concludes that future editions of *Lear* should be based on either text, but not the conflation of both. In 1931 Madeleine Doran argued a similar position in *The Text of "King Lear"* (Stanford: Stanford Univ. Press, 1931), but ten years later she retracted her belief in the authority of Q; see her review of W. W. Greg, *The Variants in the First Quarto of "King Lear." A Bibliographical and Critical Inquiry*, in *Review of English Studies* 17 (1941): 468–74. See also Steven Urkowitz, *Shakespeare's Revision of King Lear* (Princeton: Princeton Univ. Press, 1980), who argues that the Q and F texts of *Lear* represent two stages of Shakespeare's composition: the Q1 text was printed from Shakespeare's foul papers and the Folio version was printed from a quarto text that had been reconciled with the promptbook that contained Shakespeare's revisions and cuts. He illustrates his argument with detailed theatrically informed examinations of variant passages from the Q and F texts. See also Gary Taylor, "The War in *King Lear*," *Shakespeare Survey* 33 (1980): 27–34. See also nos. 189, 190, 196.

See also nos. 57, 150, 153, 166, 175, 184, 235.

F. Punctuation.

198. Alden, Raymond Macdonald. "The Punctuation of Shakespeare's Printers." *Publications of the Modern Language Association of America* 39 (1924): 557–80.

Alden considers arguments that the punctuation of the earliest printings represents the author's own expressive pointing. From an examination of numerous examples Alden argues that it is not possible to establish a systematic principle in the punctuation of the early texts, and that evidence drawn from the comparison of Folio *Merchant* with the quarto from which it was printed indicates that the Folio printers took considerable liberties with their copy. He concludes that the theories of the authorial origin of the punctuation are "Not Proven" (580).

199. Graham-White, Anthony. *Punctuation and Its Dramatic Value in Shakespearean Drama.* Newark: Univ. of Delaware Press, 1995.

Graham-White argues for a reassessment of the significance of the punctuation of the early printed texts of plays. Acknowledging that in the period of Shakespeare's writing punctuation was not standardized into a discernible system, he proposes that norms should be sought that may guide the reader and the actor concerning the oral presentation of the text; he argues that the punctuation of the early printed texts retains information obscured by modern editorial practice. His first three chapters present a brief study of the development of punctuation, a summary of the prescriptions for punctuation in grammar books in Shakespeare's time, and a description of printing house practices, with particular reference to composition and proofreading. After a discussion of punctuation in both manuscript and printed plays he presents four chapters about specific plays and playwrights. In chapter 6, "The Interpretation of Internal Evidence: Rhetoric and Character in *Richard II*" (94–104), he interprets the punctuation of Q1 *Richard II* (1597) as a guide to meaning and expression.

200. Jackson, MacD. P. "Punctuation and the Compositors of *Shakespeare's Sonnets*, 1609." *The Library*, 5th series, 30 (1975): 1–24.

Jackson presents evidence that the Q 1609 *Sonnets* was set by the two compositors who had set Q 1609 *Troilus*, Eld A and Eld B, of whom Eld B was the main compositor. He argues that the punctuation of the text is largely compositorial in origin and he discriminates Eld A's and Eld B's very different habits; however, he notes that the uneven incidence of commas apparently unrelated to compositor habits may reflect manuscript copy.

201. McKenzie, D. F. "Shakespearian Punctuation—A New Beginning." *Review of English Studies* 10 (1959): 361–70.

McKenzie notes the desire to learn more about the nature of the punctuation in the printer's copy and about the role of the compositors in punctuating the printed text. He studies as a test case the work of Jaggard's compositor B in setting the 1619 Quarto of *Merchant* from the First Quarto. He notes that of 3,200 changes that the compositor made, 715 involve punctuation, and he categorizes the various changes: the introduction of commas and parentheses; the alteration of commas to semi-colons and colons; the changing of semi-colons, colons, periods, and question marks. From his study he concludes that the compositor appears in places to act from principle but that he can also be erratic; that his behavior cannot be predicted; and that the role of the compositor in the punctuating of texts is an important consideration for editors.

202. **McKenzie, D. F.** "Stretching a Point: or, the Case of the Spaced-Out Comps." *Studies in Bibliography* 37 (1984): 106-21.

McKenzie tests the proposition (used by Shakespearean bibliographers) that compositors may be identified by their practice in spacing punctuation, specifically the placing of spaces before a comma. From an examination of the spacing of 13,777 commas in Joseph Beaumont's *Psyche* (1702) he constructs a model of the setting of the pages of the book, only to demonstrate that the records of the Cambridge University Press indicate that the pattern of spaced commas bears no relation to the historical facts of the book's composition; he further shows that no conclusions about the printing process may be drawn reliably on the basis of the relation between compositors, skeleton-formes, and press-crews.

203. **Salmon, Vivian.** "Early Seventeenth-Century Punctuation as a Guide to Sentence Structure." *Review of English Studies,* n.s., 13 (1962): 347-60. Repr. in Vivian Salmon, *The Study of Language in 17th-Century England.* Amsterdam Studies in the Theory and History of Linguistic Science, series 3—Studies in the History of Linguistics, vol. 17, 47-60. Amsterdam: John Benjamins, 1979.

In response to McKenzie (no. 201) Salmon argues that the work of Compositor B was by no means as unsystematic as McKenzie suggests. She examines the work of Henoch Clapham, who in a verse prefaced to *The Oliue Leafe* by Alexander Top (1603) records that in the role of an editor he repunctuated the author's confused manuscript. A holograph manuscript of a work by Clapham survives as an independent indicator of his principles and practice in punctuation. From the similarities between the punctuation of the two, Salmon shows that Clapham punctuated on principles that would mark the structural units of the sentence rather than rhetorical phrasing, that there is reason to presume that the compositor of *The Oliue Leafe* did follow the copy that he received, and that the system that Clapham employed is consistent with the practices that McKenzie discerned in Compositor B.

204. **Simpson, Percy.** *Shakespearian Punctuation.* Oxford: Clarendon Press, 1911.

Simpson rejects the negative view of the punctuation of the early printed

Shakespeare texts as the product of negligent compositors inattentive to the content of their copy. He argues instead that the punctuation is based on a set of principles: that where modern publication is logical and uniform, the punctuation of Shakespeare's age was "mainly rhythmical" (8). From observation of the practice in the First Folio he argues that the various occurrences of punctuation marks "admit of intelligible explanation" (11), that they reveal the "life and force of the original" (12), and that they express "subtle differences of tone" (10). For Simpson editorial repunctuation of the "on the whole sound and reasonable" (15) punctuation of the First Folio is distortion produced by the "promptings of [scholars'] fancy" (14). He presents a series of studies that indicate the customary and varied uses of comma, semi-colon, colon, and period; he takes his specific examples from the Folio and from verse and prose writers of the period including Marlowe, Dekker, and Jonson. He draws attention to the use of the period to close an incomplete sentence or to mark an interrupted speech, of the question mark to indicate an exclamation, and of the hyphen to suggest a particular metrical effect. He also proposes that the capitalization of the initial letter of a noun is a means of denoting emphasis. This book initiates the discussion of the relation of the punctuation of the printed texts to Shakespeare's practice. See also nos. 33, 198, 199, 201, 203, 205.

205. Smith, Bruce R. "Prickly Characters." In *Reading and Writing in Shakespeare*, ed. David M. Bergeron, 25-44. Newark: Univ. of Delaware Press, 1996.

Smith proposes (after Walter Ong) that punctuation is based on two principles: physiological (related to human breath patterns) and syntactical (related to grammatical structures). He argues that the punctuation of the Hand D passage of *More* is exclusively physiological, and that that of the "To be" soliloquy in *Hamlet* Q2 and F1 is also. He then demonstrates how the repunctuation by successive editors becomes increasingly syntactical and that that of the Oxford Shakespeare is exclusively syntactical.

See also nos. 34, 71, 78, 79, 107, 112, 221, 230, 231, 237.

G. Editorial Theory and Practice.

206. Black, Matthew W., and Matthias A. Shaaber. *Shakespeare's Seventeenth-Century Editors 1632-1685*. New York: Modern Language Association of America, 1937.

Black and Shaaber collect and study all the variants that they can find in F2, F3, and F4. After establishing working criteria for distinguishing whether a textual change is the result of chance or intention, they conclude that F2 contains 1,679 deliberate editorial changes from F1, that F3 contains 943 editorial changes from F2, and F4 751 editorial changes from F3; none of the changes is a consequence of systematic collation with quarto texts. They conjecture that for the preparation of F2 a specially qualified editor was employed to mark up a copy of F1, but that for F3 and F4 the changes were probably made on the proof sheets and that the editors were professional proof correctors. Black and Shaaber argue that these early editors should be considered as having practiced textual criticism on their copy, and that F2, F3, and F4 are as much critical editions as Rowe's edition, although they grant that none of these folios has authority in determining the text of any play. They propose that the editor of F2 should be considered the first of Shakespeare's editors, and they accord him high praise. The main body of the book is a record of all the editorial changes detected in F2, F3, and F4.

207. Bowers, Fredson. *On Editing Shakespeare and the Elizabethan Dramatists.* Philadelphia: Univ. of Pennsylvania Press, 1955. Repr., with additions, as *On Editing Shakespeare.* Charlottesville: Univ. Press of Virginia, 1966.

In the first three chapters, the Rosenbach Lectures of 1954 that constitute the book printed in 1955, Bowers discusses the importance for editing of the discrimination of the nature of the copy that went to the printer, the knowledge of the process in the printing shop, and the relation between all preserved examples of a text and the relative authority among them. Rejecting the idea that plays were printed only either from foul papers or from promptbooks, he specifies thirteen possible derivations of printer's copy; he further asserts that playwrights provided acting companies with fair copy of their plays. Bowers stresses the importance of the identification of compositors for the editorial establishment of text. Chapter 4, "What Shakespeare Wrote" (reprinted from *Shakespeare Jahrbuch*, 98 [1962]: 24–50), reviews particular problems of editorial discrimination. Chapter 5, "Today's Shakespeare Texts, and Tomorrow's" (reprinted from *Studies in Bibliography* 19 [1966]: 39–65), presents a history of editions since Clark and Wright's Cambridge edition of 1863–66 (no. 144), argues the case for modernizing punctuation in modern-spelling editions, advocates the preparation of an old-spelling critical edition, and considers the problems of knowledge that remain to be addressed. See also Fredson Bowers, *Textual and Literary Criticism* (Cambridge: Cambridge Univ. Press, 1959).

208. De Grazia, Margreta. "The Essential Shakespeare and the Material Book." *Textual Practice* 2 (1988): 69–86.

De Grazia argues that the new attention to the material book characteristic of the New Bibliography was paradoxically notable for its anti-materialist or idealist strain, the pursuit of the essential Shakespeare beyond the material phenomena. She argues that the scientific method of the New Bibliographers, grounded in the discrimination of Good from Bad Quartos and in the establishment of textual lineage, serves in their work and of that of their successors to restore a lost authorial manuscript by the editorial production of a purely authorial "incarnational" text (82). She calls for an examination of the book as a material object, separate from the constraining pursuit of the authorial original and an authorial meaning.

209. De Grazia, Margreta, and Peter Stallybrass. "The Materiality of the Shakespearean Text." *Shakespeare Quarterly* 44 (1993): 255–83. Repr. in Orgel and Keilen (no. 238).

In denying any transcendental authorial figure or state of a work, De Grazia and Stallybrass insist upon the material nature of the extant textual object. They discuss the absence of self-identity of any work, citing the multiple states in which works survive; they comment on the problems involved in interpreting the spelling of words; they argue against conventional ways of discussing character, attending to the instability of speech headings; they suggest that the category of author misrepresents the nature of practices of composition. In the light of their insistence on the absence of identifiable originals outside the material remains, they conclude by justifying the practice of editorial modernizing.

210. De Grazia, Margreta. *Shakespeare Verbatim: The Reproduction of Authenticity and the 1790 Apparatus.* Oxford: Clarendon Press, 1991.

De Grazia studies Malone's 1790 edition of Shakespeare (see nos. 35, 147) as marking a significant moment in the history of Shakespearean scholarship when textual and critical approaches changed demonstrably. She argues that fundamental principles and practices that underlie two centuries of succeeding work are exemplified for the first time in Malone's edition: in his establishment of a new criterion of authenticity he introduced a scientific historical attitude into textual and biographical studies, which she relates to various aspects of Enlightenment thinking. De Grazia illustrates the diverse nature of his radical departure. She demonstrates how, in aiming to restore the "original" text of each play by an examination of the earliest printed evidence, Malone broke with the general habits of previous editors, whose approach to the text was dominated by the accommodations of their contemporary taste. She argues that he replaced literary judgment by factual scholarship, not least in his observation of distinctive features of Shakespeare's language and in his establishment of a chronology of the composition of the works; she notes how he introduced the distinction between internal and external evidence into Shakespeare studies. She asserts that the format of Malone's edition reinforced the identification of the text with the individual mind of Shakespeare and that the apparatus worked to authorize the text, providing rules for reading. De Grazia shows that the same authenticating impulse is apparent in his treatment of the life, with his dismissal of the traditional tales and his dependence on archival records; she is particularly acute on the subject of the treatment of the *Sonnets* prior to Malone's edition, not least with regard to his introduction of the concept of Shakespeare's interiority as evident in the poems, and on the relation of changes in the conception of copyright to Malone's construction of Shakespeare as author and of his text.

211. Dillon, Janette. "Is There a Performance in this Text?" *Shakespeare Quarterly* 45 (1994): 74–86.

Focussing on arguments of Graham Holderness and Bryan Loughrey in their edition of Q1 *Hamlet, The Tragicall Historie of Hamlet Prince of Denmarke* (Hemel Hempstead: Harvester Wheatsheaf, 1992), Dillon rejects the instatement of performance as the measure of textual "authenticity" to replace the no longer valid category of the author. She argues that studies that place high value on Q1 *Hamlet* because it is a "performance text" do not recognize the variety of performances produced from a text in Jacobean times, and should not constitute a new ideal form, the text for the Jacobean stage, to replace the older authorial ideal. She asserts the need to study surviving texts as distinct entities whose material nature requires skeptical unromantic examination.

212. Foakes, R. A. "Shakespeare Editing and Textual Theory: A Rough Guide." *Huntington Library Quarterly* 60 (1999): 425–42.

Foakes provides an overview of the theoretical controversies concerning Shakespearean textual scholarship particularly as they relate to editing. He discusses concepts such as the author, materiality, instability, editing and unediting, and intention. His survey of the contemporary scene is from the position of the editor whose task is to establish a text that will provide a broad reading public as well as scholarly readers with a representation of Shakespeare's intentions and that will serve also as a theatrical script. He suggests that materialist theoretical concerns have little relevance to editorial practice, arguing that in cases of multiplicity of textual states, readers need editorial guidance.

213. Greg, W. W. *The Editorial Problem in Shakespeare.* Oxford: Clarendon Press, 1942. 2nd edition, 1951; 3rd edition, 1954.

The Clark Lectures for 1939, delivered before the publication of McKerrow's *Prolegomena* (no. 222), are preceded by Greg's own Prolegomena, in which he advances seven rules for editorial practice. Sharing McKerrow's conception of the "ideal text," Greg complicates the idea of "substantive" and "derivative" texts, arguing for the possibility of more than one authoritative text of a play; he rejects McKerrow's conservative concept of fidelity to the copy-text, proposing that an eclectic principle is justified in situations of multiple authority where authorial traces are detectable in more than one text, although he dismisses the likelihood of revision in Shakespeare. He emphasizes the problematic nature of the editor's determination of relative authority. In the lectures he presents the state of knowledge of theatrical manuscripts. He then discusses the texts of the individual Bad Quartos as products of memorial reconstruction; of *Richard III* and *Lear*, which he classes as Doubtful Quartos; of the Good Quartos, the copy for each of which he designates as foul papers or an immediately derived manuscript; of the plays that appear first in the First Folio, for which he proposes various origins. There is an appendix of illustrative stage directions and a final summary and table of his conclusions concerning the copy for each play. The preface to the second edition records Greg's rethinking of many points in the light of new knowledge; that to the third edition refers to a few corrections and updatings of references. See also no. 232.

214. Greg, W. W. "Principles of Emendation in Shakespeare." *Proceedings of the British Academy* 14 (1928): 147–216. Published separately, London: Oxford Univ. Press, 1928.

After declaring that emendation is an art and not a science, Greg investigates the conditions that make an emendation acceptable; he insists that emendation must be considered in the context of the origins and history of the text and not *"in vacuo"* (152). Dividing the Shakespeare texts into four groups according to their early printing history, he reviews specific cruxes and the history of their treatment, paying particular attention to examples from *2 Henry IV*, *Troilus*, *Othello*, *Lear*, *Henry V*, *Romeo*, and *Hamlet*. The extensive notes contain discussions of numerous other passages. For a further discussion of the art of emendation, specifically of passages where an omission from the text is suspected, see also Gary Taylor, "Inventing Shakespeare," *Shakespeare Jahrbuch West* (1986): 26–44.

215. Greg, W. W. "The Rationale of Copy-Text." *Studies In Bibliography* 3 (1950): 19–36. Repr. in *Collected Papers*, ed. J. C. Maxwell (no. 153), 374–91.

Discriminating the principles that should govern the editing of printed works from those characteristic of the editing of classical literature deriving from a manuscript tradition, Greg argues against an absolute fidelity to the readings of that text selected to be the copy-text of a work. He proposes a distinction between substantives and accidentals (21); he argues that, in establishing an old-spelling text of a work existing in more than one authoritative state, the editor should accept the authority of the copy-text in accidentals only, and with respect to substantives should choose between variant readings on critical principles rather than follow the copy-text exclusively; he thus rejects "the tyranny of the copy-text" (26). He proposes further that in cases where readings from a second text or emendations are introduced into the old-spelling text, the new readings should conform in spelling to that of the copy-text. See no. 232.

216. Holderness, Graham, Bryan Loughrey, and Andrew Murphy. "'What's the Matter?' Shakespeare and Textual Theory." *Textual Practice* 9 (1995): 93–119.

The authors survey the response to the New Bibliography manifested in the editorial practices and theoretical writings of the "New Textualists," represented by De Grazia (no. 208), De Grazia and Stallybrass (no. 209), Wells and Taylor (no. 169), Goldberg (no. 189), Orgel (nos. 227, 228), Jerome McGann, and Michael Warren. They argue that behind the ostensible attention of these revisionist thinkers to the material texts there lies either a persisting attachment to the idea of the author or a poststructuralist celebration of textual uncertainty. Both these positions, they argue, distract from the need for a true materialist approach to printed objects as products of cultural work.

217. Honigmann, E. A. J. "Re-Enter the Stage Direction: Shakespeare and Some Contemporaries." *Shakespeare Survey* 29 (1976): 117–26.

Honigmann addresses the form of stage directions in the earliest printed texts and their treatment in modern critical editions. He discusses the placing of entrances and actions in relation to lines referring to them and advocates a standardization of editorial practice; criticizes the excessive introduction of the term "aside"; studies the problems relating to the speech headings "All" and "Both," recommending principles for their retention or emendation; advocates the replacement of nonverbal sounds ("Cryptodirections") by descriptive statements; and urges comparative studies of various authors to understand contemporary practice better. See also Alan C. Dessen, *Recovering Shakespeare's Dramatic Language* (Cambridge: Cambridge Univ. Press, 1995).

218. Jowett, John. "After Oxford: Recent developments in textual studies." In *The Shakespearean International Yearbook. 1. Where are we now in Shakespeare studies?*, ed. W. R. Elton and John M. Mucciolo, 65–86. Aldershot, U.K.: Ashgate, 1999.

Jowett discusses the state of textual studies at the end of the century. He begins from the impact of revision theory and the destabilization of text upon the principles of the New Bibliography, discussing the Oxford Shakespeare *Complete Works* (Oxford: Oxford Univ. Press, 1986) as an edition exemplifying the tension between canonicity and fragmentation—the text available in old- and modern-spelling formats, the apparatus and documentation in a separate volume, a *Textual Companion* (no. 169). He explores the implications of postmodern thought for editing, considering topics such as emendation, the modernization of spelling and punctuation, the regularization of speech headings, the concept of the author, the relation of performance to texts, and the status of Bad Quartos. He surveys the varied qualities of current series of Shakespeare editions and ends with a contemplation of the impact and possible future role of electronic formats, particularly in relation to the preparation of new electronic editions.

219. Marcus, Leah S. *Unediting the Renaissance: Shakespeare, Marlowe, Milton*. London: Routledge, 1996.

In an introductory chapter Marcus describes recent shifts in the paradigm of textual studies, specifically addressing the recent challenge of materialist thinking to the New Bibliography's concern with the singular and ideal edited text. In separate chapters she discusses the relations of Q and F *Merry Wives*, of *A Shrew* and *The Shrew*, and of Q1, Q2, and F *Hamlet*. Using anthropological ideas of purity and danger, she demonstrates how editors reject texts and readings in the pursuit of textual purity while they are influenced by their own desires to construct a particular text as valid. In each study she examines comparatively the distinctive features of the various texts. Rejecting current editorial practice, she argues pervasively for the acceptance of a multiplicity of surviving texts that are intertextually related.

220. Masten, Jeffrey. *Textual Intercourse: Collaboration, Authorship, and Sexualities in Renaissance Drama*. Cambridge: Cambridge Univ. Press, 1996.

Masten asserts initially that collaboration dominated as the mode of authorship during the time of Shakespeare and Beaumont and Fletcher, and that "textual production ... occurred within the context of conflicting and contested 'sex/gender systems'" (4). He proposes that collaboration should be considered not as a distribution of isolated responsibilities in a text to independent individuals, but as a corporate activity in which there is no distinguishable authorship. He shows also how in the early seventeenth century a concept of "the author" emerged, conceived in patriarchal-absolutist terms; he suggests that the Jonson and Shakespeare folios were an important factor in this development. Masten's primary focus is on the Beaumont and Fletcher plays, but he draws evidence from the Shakespeare plays and attends to the image of the author in *Pericles* and *Tempest*. Douglas Brooks also discusses the concept of "the author" in relation to Shakespeare in the context of collaborative writing and of publishing practices in *From Playhouse to Printing House: Drama and Authorship in Early Modern England* (Cambridge: Cambridge Univ. Press, 2000).

221. McKenzie, D. F. "Printers of the Mind: Some Notes On Bibliographical Theories and Printing-House Practices." *Studies in Bibliography* 22 (1969): 1–75.

McKenzie challenges the principles and conclusions of scientific bibliography, particularly as represented by the work of Bowers and Hinman. He demonstrates from the records of Cambridge University Press and other printing houses that the practice of printers was so various as not to be susceptible of the generalizations of the scientific bibliographers: he finds concurrent production of more than one book to be the norm and proves that compositors worked regularly on more than one project. He argues further that Hinman's conception of proofreading (see nos. 136, 159) is in error because he fails to take into account the practice of reading a proof sheet before printing begins, and that Hinman's records are of stop-press correction after an earlier proof had been read. Although the evidence McKenzie uses is from a later date than that of Shakespeare's printers, he argues that the basic practices of the printers of the two periods were more likely to resemble each other than to differ.

222. McKerrow, R. B. *Prolegomena for the Oxford Shakespeare: A Study in Historical Method.* Oxford: Clarendon Press, 1939.

McKerrow articulates the editorial policy for his projected old-spelling collected works. He defines the "ideal text" as "one which ... should approach as closely as the extant material allows to a fair copy, made by the author himself, of his plays in the form which he intended finally to give them" (6). He distinguishes the roles of "substantive" and "derived" texts and the relative qualities of "most authoritative" texts and "most correct" texts. He argues for the conservative treatment of the copy-text with regard to spelling, punctuation, and grammatical irregularities, for minimal alteration of stage directions, but for regularization of speech headings.

He describes the principles of his collations and the nature of his notes. He outlines a plan for through line numbering based on the First Folio text. See no. 232.

223. McKerrow, Ronald B. "The Treatment of Shakespeare's Text by his Earliest Editors, 1709–1768." *Proceedings of the British Academy* 19 (1933): 89–122. Published separately, London: H. Milford, 1933. Repr. in *Studies in Shakespeare. British Academy Lectures*, ed. Peter Alexander, 103–31. Oxford: Oxford Univ. Press, 1964.

After a brief summary of the process of reprinting of folios and quartos in the seventeenth century, McKerrow reviews the practice of eighteenth-century editors with particular attention to the editions of Rowe, Pope, Theobald, Johnson, and Capell, describing the texts to which they had access and the characteristics of the work of each. He argues that despite the increased availabilty of quarto texts the later editors produced eclectic texts like those of their predecessors because they lacked a theory of the descent of the text, treating each printing as an individual authority (after the manner of the scholarship of classical manuscripts) and not as part of a distinguishable sequence where reprints have no authority.

224. McLeod, Randall. "Spellbound: Typography and the Concept of Old-Spelling Editions." *Renaissance and Reformation*, n.s., 3 (1979): 50–65. Repr. in *Play-Texts in Old Spelling*, ed. G. B. Shand and Raymond C. Shady. New York: AMS Press, 1984.

McLeod argues that the spelling of words in early printing is often a product of exigencies in the setting of type, and that consequently spelling has limits as an indication of compositorial practice. He describes how the form of a word may be caused by the compositor's desire to avoid damage to kerning types (pieces of type of which a part—the kern—extends outside the type body) by the introduction of an additional medial letter or a hyphen, or may result from the necessity of justifying the line. He argues further that the absence from the textual apparatus in editions of evidence of the use of long "s" and of ligatures withholds important information and misrepresents the textual condition.

225. McLeod, Randall. "UN*Editing* Shak-speare." *Sub-Stance* 33/34 (1982): 26–55. Repr. in Orgel and Keilen (no. 238).

After an initial meditation on Keats's reading of *Lear* and the variant states of his sonnet "On Sitting Down to [Read] King Lear Once Again," McLeod stresses the iconicity of texts, arguing for the importance of photographic facsimiles as enabling the treatment of the textual object as object. In the succeeding argument about Shakespeare he argues for the theoretical necessity of the separate identity of Q and F *Lear*, rejecting the practice of editorial conflation, and for the preservation of the material text's punctuation. McLeod observes that the preservation of old spelling in edited texts conceals the function of exigencies of type in determining spelling. He draws attention to the limitations of *The Harvard Concordance to Shakespeare* (no. 26), from which titles, speech headings, stage directions, dialogue in stage directions, and arguments to poems are excluded. He draws attention to the regularizing force of lists of dramatis personae and also to editors' custom of regularizing all speech headings, which renders tidy the unruly existential text.

226. Mowat, Barbara A. "The Problem of Shakespeare's Text(s)." *Shakespeare Jahrbuch* 132 (1996): 26–43.

Mowat argues that recent research has made impossible the identification of the manuscript copy behind each printing of a Shakespeare play, and that the objective of recovering the lost authorial manuscript is always an illusion; she cites the works of other authors whose multiple manuscripts and variant printed states indicate a text in constant flux. She proposes that the editor's "problem" is "no longer so much theoretical as practical," and that the editor should simply reproduce as closely as possible the printed text chosen to be the basis of the edition, introducing variants and emendations "only in specific circumstances" that are to be explained in the textual introduction (43). See no. 232, and also W. Speed Hill, "Where are the Bibliographers of Yesteryear?" in *Pilgrimage for Love: Essays in Early Modern Literature in Honor of Josephine A. Roberts*, ed. Sigrid King, 115–32 (Tempe, Ariz.: Arizona Center for Medieval and Renaissance Studies, 1999).

227. Orgel, Stephen. "The Authentic Shakespeare." *Representations* 21 (1988): 1–25. Repr. in Orgel and Keilen (no. 238).

In discussing the concept of authentication of what is "Shakespeare," Orgel argues that the editor's pursuit of the "authentic" Shakespeare text is an illusion. Citing the three texts of *Hamlet* as an example, he observes that texts, like performances, were fluid in Shakespeare's time; he notes also how individual copies of books varied one from another. He suggests that in composing a play Shakespeare always wrote more than the playing company needed, and that the creation of the performance text was a collaborative act with the company.

228. Orgel, Stephen. "What is a Text?" *Research Opportunities in Renaissance Drama* 24 (1981): 3–6. Repr. in *Staging the Renaissance*, ed. David Scott Kastan and Peter Stallybrass. London: Routledge, 1991.

Following Gerald Eades Bentley's discussion of the role of dramatists in *The Profession of Dramatist in Shakespeare's Time* (Princeton: Princeton Univ. Press, 1971), Orgel argues that the commercial conditions under which writers wrote plays and the treatment of the play in the playhouse, where it would be modified by the company for performance, make all composition of plays in the period essentially a collaborative enterprise and call into question the "author's" relation to the text; he rejects the idea of Shakespeare as a special case, suggesting that because of his role in the company he would merely be a participant in more aspects of the process. He also argues (after Honigmann, no. 191) for the fundamental instability of all texts in the light of persistent rewriting by authors or others, and against the idea that editions reconstitute the author's original text, because such a text is irrecoverable, given the presence of intermediaries in the creation of the play and its transmission.

229. Trousdale, Marion. "Diachronic and Synchronic: Critical Bibliography and the Acting of Plays." In *Shakespeare: Text, Language, Criticism: Essays in Honor of Marvin Spevack*, ed. Bernhard Fabian and Kurt Tetzeli von Rosador, 304–14. Hildesheim, Germany: Olms-Weidmann, 1987.

Trousdale discerns in the theoretical writings of McKerrow and Greg a desire to evolve principles on the basis of the accumulated data about early printed texts; she notes the conflict between the aspiration to science and the experience of the necessity of judgment. She then examines the paradox of editing as manifested in the statements of Stanley Wells (see no. 231), who expresses the desire both to conserve and yet simultaneously make accessible to the modern reader material of remote origin. Trousdale thus notes the editorial striving for certainty in a situation of unavoidable uncertainty, the unstable world of the origin of Shakespeare's texts.

230. Wells, Stanley. *Modernizing Shakespeare's Spelling* (with Gary Taylor, *Three Studies in the Text of "Henry V"*). Oxford: Clarendon Press, 1979.

In *Modernizing* Wells reviews the many problems that the editor confronts in creating a modern-spelling text and indicates the principles on which the Oxford Shakespeare is to be prepared. He argues that an editor cannot responsibly be half-hearted in his/her approach, and yet he acknowledges that exceptions must be made in many kinds of situations. Wells rejects the retention of archaic forms where there are semantically indifferent variants, examines the challenges that semantically significant variants present, and discusses exceptions, for instance, for the preservation of rhyme and for the representation of dialect forms. He explores the demands of contracted forms, especially in relation to meter. He notes the impossibility of a single formulation for the treatment of proper names and concludes with a discussion of the modernizing of punctuation; he accepts the obligation to diminish the potential for imposing interpretation upon the text and proposes the sparing introduction of stops such as semi-colons, colons, and exclamation marks.

231. Wells, Stanley. *Re-Editing Shakespeare for the Modern Reader.* Oxford: Clarendon Press, 1984.

Wells discusses the practical issues that confront the editor of Shakespeare's texts. In four chapters he justifies the preparation of modernized texts and proposes solutions for the many problems that they raise; explains the various circumstances that occasion emendation and proposes specific emendations; reviews the treatment of stage directions (the provision and location of exits and entrances, for instance); and concludes with an elaborate demonstration of the difficulties attendant upon editing act 1 of *Titus*, including in an appendix a conjectural reconstruction of Shakespeare's "first draft." Margaret Jane Kidnie challenges Wells's treatment of stage directions in "Text, Performance, and Editors: Staging Shakespeare's Drama," *Shakespeare Quarterly* 51 (2000): 456–73.

232. Werstine, Paul. "Editing Shakespeare and Editing Without Shakespeare: Wilson, McKerrow, Greg, Bowers, Tanselle, and Copy-Text Editing," *TEXT* 13 (2000): 27–53.

Werstine discusses the consequences for current editors of the loss of authorial presence, the decentering of Shakespeare; he reviews the evidence for the impossibility of discriminating the origins of printed texts in foul papers or promptbooks, and he notes the challenges to the identification of Hand D of *More* as Shakespeare's. He then examines in detail the positions of McKerrow in *Prolegomena* (no. 222) and Greg in *Editorial Problem* (no. 213) and "Rationale" (no. 215) concerning these issues, and argues that the standard narrative of the origin of the theory of copy-text editing suppresses McKerrow's skepticism about Greg's confidence in the detection of the origin of printers' copy. Werstine suggests that McKerrow's dissent from Greg, his advocacy of a "pragmatic strategy for editing, rather than a theoretically rigorous and hence utterly impracticable agenda" (52), represents a debate similar to that conducted in current editorial theory. See also no. 225.

See also nos. 131, 143, 144, 147, 148, 153, 163, 164, 165, 189, 191, 233, 234, 235, 236, 237, 237a, 238, 239, 240, 241.

H. Recent Collections of Essays.

233. Cox, John D., and David Scott Kastan, eds. *A New History of Early English Drama.* New York: Columbia Univ. Press, 1997.

This collection contains four essays relating to Shakespearean texts: Jeffrey Masten, "Playwrighting: Authorship and Collaboration" (357–82); Peter W. M. Blayney, "The Publication of Playbooks" (383–422); Eric Rasmussen, "The Revision of Scripts" (441–60); and Paul Werstine, "Plays in Manuscript" (481–97). Masten argues the need to reconceive collaboration; in the context of philological reassessments of key terms in use in the sixteenth and seventeenth centuries, he proposes that common conceptions misrepresent the widespread corporate rather than individualist culture of playwrights and playhouses. Blayney provides a thorough and precisely argued summary of contemporary practices in the publication of plays, clarifying the roles of printer, publisher, and bookseller, the nature of "authority" and "license," and providing an analysis of the probable economics of the printing of a play in quarto. Although Blayney admits that much in his reconstruction is hypothetical, his narrative is comprehensive and he successfully challenges the myth of piracy that originated with Pollard (see no. 183). Rasmussen argues that the production process inevitably led to changes in the authorial text tantamount to revision; he then examines the various forms of observable revision, exposing the difficulty of distinguishing alterations originating with the author from those made by a book-keeper. He concludes by discussing the implications for editing of his ideas. Werstine discusses the way in which Greg evolved his theory of kinds of dramatic documents not as a result of an extensive survey of all known documents but primarily as a response to the arguments of Lee (no. 161) and Pollard (no. 183). He subjects the concept of "foul papers" to stringent examination, arguing that no convincing example of foul papers has been discovered, and proposes that Greg's narrative of the transmission of playhouse documents to printers (see nos. 156, 213) should be abandoned.

234. "Forum: Editing Early Modern Texts." *Shakespeare Studies* 24 (1996): 19–78.

This collection of six commissioned essays addresses the challenge of postmodern thought to the practice of textual editing. Four scholars address directly issues concerning the editing of Shakespeare texts. In "What is an Editor" (23–29, and repr. in Orgel and Keilen, no. 238) Stephen Orgel reviews the problems for editors of the instability of texts, which he insists should be considered not as ideas but as artifacts; he notes that variant states of particular books render facsimiles as limited and faulty as editions.

David Scott Kastan ("The Mechanics of Culture: Editing Shakespeare Today," 30-37, repr. in Orgel and Keilen, no. 238) reviews the problems associated with editing's abstraction of plays from the material conditions of their cultural production and with the concept of authorship. He comments on the "impossibility of editing and yet the inescapability of it" (37). In "Where We Are and How We Got Here: Editing after Poststructuralism" (38-46), W. Speed Hill discusses the various forms editions can now take—multiple version, socialized, hypertext, generic, and facsimile —in a world of the decentered author and the suspicion of the unitary text. Paul Werstine writes as an apologist for and a practitioner of poststructuralist editing ("Editing after the End of Editing," 47-54). After a brief history of twentieth-century editorial thought, especially in relation to the concept of the author, he discusses techniques and formats for editing that he suggests address the challenges of postmodern thought. In a fifth essay John Pitcher argues "Why Editors Should Write More Notes" (55-62), stating that current editions do not elucidate or illuminate verbal details sufficiently. Susan Zimmerman provides a foreword and an afterword.

235. Kastan, David Scott, ed. *A Companion to Shakespeare.* Oxford: Blackwell, 1999.

In part 7, on printing, five essays appear. Thomas L. Berger and Jesse M. Lander ("Shakespeare in Print, 1593-1640," 395-413) provide a brisk summary of the publication of the poems, plays in quarto, the First Folio, the 1640 *Poems*, and later folios. In "'Precious Few': English Manuscript Playbooks" (414-33) William B. Long dispels myths about playbooks of the period and describes the characteristics of each of those that are extant. The practices of the printing house of the time are described by Laurie E. Maguire in "The Craft of Printing (1600)" (434-49). Mark Bland surveys a representative year in both print and manuscript publishing in "The London Book-Trade in 1600" (450-63). Cyndia Susan Clegg discusses the practice of press censorship in relation to Shakespeare's works in "Liberty, License, and Authority: Press Censorship and Shakespeare" (464-85). She asserts that to identify definitely the operation of censorship on Shakespearean printed texts is difficult; however, she proposes that "the one instance where press censorship seems altogether likely" (479) is the initial quarto publication of *Richard II* in 1597.

236. Maguire, Laurie E., and Thomas L. Berger, eds. *Textual Formations and Reformations.* Newark: Univ. of Delaware Press, 1998.

Several of the 13 essays in this collection address directly issues concerning the Shakespearean texts. In "Authentic Reproductions: The Material Origins of the New Bibliography" (23–44), Joseph F. Loewenstein relates the function of the term author in the New Bibliography and specifically in the work of Greg and Pollard to changes in the Copyright Law of 1911. Paul Werstine ("Touring and the Construction of Shakespeare Criticism," 45–66) reviews the origin and history of the category Bad Quartos and posits that there is no evidence that links them to performance in the provinces or in London. A. R. Braunmuller discusses problems of editorial intervention and correction with particular relation to *Macbeth* in "How farre is't called to Soris? or, Where was Mr. Hobbs when Charles II died?" (112–30). In "The Problem of Shakespeare's Text(s)" (131–48), a "different version" (148) of no. 226, Barbara A. Mowat attacks editors' desire to recreate the lost authorial manuscript, arguing that the record of holograph manuscripts of other authors suggests that such a single point of origin does not normally exist; she proposes that in a post-New Bibliography world the restoration of true readings and recreation of the authorial manuscript are false objectives. David Scott Kastan (" 'Killed with Hard Opinions': Oldcastle, Falstaff, and the Reformed Text of *1 Henry IV*," 211–27) examines the significance of the Oxford Shakespeare's substitution of Oldcastle for Falstaff in *1 Henry IV* and concludes that it manifests the idealization of the author and the rejection of the complex social history of the text. In "*The Taming of a Shrew* and the Theories; or, 'Though this be badness, yet there is method in't'" (251–63), Stephen Miller presents a history of the criticism of *A Shrew* and argues for its being the work of an adapter of *The Shrew*.

237. M Leod, Randall (McLeod, Randall), ed. *Crisis in Editing: Texts of the English Renaissance.* New York: AMS Press, 1994.

Four of the six articles in this collection relate directly to Shakespeare. Gary Taylor, "The Rhetorics of Reaction" (19–59) analyzes the role of rhetoric in textual debate, particularly that concerning revision, and argues that it is pervasive and unavoidable; he demonstrates that it is as present in the arguments of reactionary critics as in those of critics whom they condemn as merely depending on rhetoric. In " 'What? in a names that which we call a Rose,' The Desired Texts of *Romeo and Juliet*" (173–201, and repr. in Orgel and Keilen, no. 238) Jonathan Goldberg argues that the variations in surviving texts of plays indicate a fundamental uncertainty surrounding the "original" text; he concludes that bibliographic logic masks the operations of the editor's intellectual desire for a phantasm. From an examination of a variety of manuscript and print documents Antony Hammond argues in "Searching for the Signal in Renaissance Dramatic Texts" (203–4) that punctuation was initially a distinctive feature of printed texts rather than of playhouse materials. He suggests that in the Jacobean and Caroline periods authors came to use more punctuation in manuscripts as a means of exercising artistic control. Using the Padua Promptbooks and the reports of Simon Forman as evidence, Stephen Orgel, "Acting Scripts, Performing Texts" (252–94), demonstrates the difference between the printed text and what was performed onstage. After discussing the editorial treatment of a number of passages in which there is uncertainty whether the text is in prose or verse, he asserts that the instability of the texts validates them as useful representations of earlier theatrical experience.

237a. Murphy, Andrew, ed. *The Renaissance Text: Theory, editing, textuality*. Manchester and New York: Manchester Univ. Press, 2000.

Several essays concern Shakespeare texts directly. In "(Un)Editing and textual theory: positioning the reader" (73–90), Michael Steppat discusses the rhetorical strategies of textual criticism, addressing specifically Leah S. Marcus's *Unediting the Renaissance* (no. 219). Peter Stallybrass examines the naming of characters in speech headings, stage directions, and spoken text in quartos and the First Folio and subsequent editions, relating his findings to changing conceptions of social identity and private individuality ("Naming, renaming and unnaming in the Shakespearean quartos and folio," 108–34). Laurie E. Maguire ("Composition/decomposition: singular Shakespeare and the death of the author," 135–53) considers, with particular reference to the First Folio and to the concept of memorial reconstruction, the role of memory and the creation of memorials in the practice of editing; she describes the establishment of singular "ideal" texts as a form of mourning the loss of the author and the recognition and perpetuation of textual multiplicity as a revitalization of the author. Graham Holderness, Stanley E. Porter, and Carol Banks compare the productions of the First Folio and the King James Bible ("Biblebable," 154–76). In "Ghost writing: *Hamlet* and the Ur-Hamlet" (177–90), Emma Smith discusses the critical and editorial history of the concept of the Ur-*Hamlet*. Andrew Murphy reviews the history of textual culture in which Shakespeare has been located, from the circumstances of oral performance and print publication in his time to the print culture of editing and the prospects for electronic editions ("Texts and textualities: a Shakespearean history," 191–210). Three papers not specifically related to Shakespeare discuss electronic editing. In "Afterword: Confessions of a reformed uneditor" (211–16), Leah S. Marcus discusses editorial policy and practice in relation to works surviving in multiple texts (in this instance, the writings and speeches of Queen Elizabeth) and to the modernization of spelling and punctuation. Marcus advocates the exploration of the potential of electronic editing, as does Graham D. Caie in "Hypertext and multiplicity: the medieval example" (30–43). Gary

Taylor presents a salutary warning about its technical perils in "c:\wp\file.txt 05:41 10-07-98" (44-54).

238. Orgel, Stephen, and Sean Keilen, eds. *Shakespeare and the Editorial Tradition.* New York and London: Garland Publishing, 1999.

This collection includes 18 previously published essays reproduced in photographic facsimile, the earliest from 1972. The subjects range from the materiality of the text, to the conception of authorship, to issues in editing such as emendation and repunctuation, and to the textual criticism of particular plays. The articles include several cited elsewhere in this bibliography: De Grazia and Stallybrass (no. 209), McLeod (no. 225), Orgel (227, 234), Taylor (see no. 214), Kastan (no. 234), Goldberg (no. 237), and McMillin (no. 182). This volume provides a very good introduction to general and particular issues in the field at the end of the twentieth century.

239. Parker, R. B., and S. P. Zitner, eds. *Elizabethan Theater: Essays in Honor of S. Schoenbaum.* Newark: Univ. of Delaware Press, 1996.

Three essays in this collection address the concept of author in relation to Shakespeare. In "The Birth of the Author" (71-92), Richard Dutton argues that Shakespeare should not be constructed solely as a man of the theater but as a literary author also; he argues that the printed texts of many of the plays were too long for performance and therefore must be considered apart from the constraints of the playhouse. Barbara A. Mowat in "Constructing the Author" (93-110) argues from evidence concerning the treatment in Shakespeare's time of Homer, Livy, and Chaucer, that the concept of the author as a "larger-than-life Creator of Works" (106) was current in the period and that the symptomatic language is present in the introductory matter of F1. In "Is There a Shakespeare after the *New* New Bibliography?" (169-83), Meredith Skura takes issue with theorists such as Orgel and De Grazia who dismiss the concept of the author; without denying the operation of other collaborative agents she argues for an identifiable originating consciousness, citing in support the incidence in plays such as *Love's Labour's, The Shrew, Dream, Merry Wives, As You Like It, Tempest,* and *Hamlet* of an image cluster that links hunting with moments related to the performance of plays.

240. Thompson, Ann, and Keir Elam, eds. *Shakespeare's Text(s). Textus: English Studies in Italy* 9 (1996): various pages.

Ten essays (by Giorgio Melchiori, David Scott Kastan, Stanley Wells, Graham Holderness and Bryan Loughrey, Lois Potter, Gordon McMullan, Alessandro Serpieri, Neil Taylor and Ann Thompson, Sonia Massai, and Stefania Magnoni) address various subjects concerning the Shakespearean texts. Most notably, McMullan ("'Our Whole Life is Like a Play': Collaboration and the Problem of Editing," 437-60) argues that "collaboration is the paradigmatic mode of textual production" (454) in the period, and rejects not just earlier conceptions of authorship but models of collaboration based on scenic distribution also. In a similar vein Kastan ("Shakespeare after Theory," 357-74) advocates the abandonment of concentration upon authorship in favor of recognition of the complex social origins of the material text; this essay is reprinted in a revised and enlarged form as chapter 1 of Kastan, *Shakespeare after Theory* (London: Routledge, 1999, 23-42). Wells ("Multiple Texts and the Oxford Shakespeare," 375-92) discusses the challenges that multiple text plays present to editors and describes their treatment in the Oxford Shakespeare. Holderness and Loughrey ("Shakespeare Misconstrued: The True Chronicle Historie of *Shakespearean Originals*," 393-418) present a statement of their objectives in their series "Shakespearean Originals" (diplomatic editions of the earliest printed texts), a history of the series' critical reception, and an answer to their critics.

241. Williams, George Walton, ed. *Shakespeare's Speech-Headings.* Newark: University of Delaware Press, 1997.

Williams introduces this collection of essays, deriving from a Shakespeare Association of America seminar held in 1986, with a preface in which he summarizes the issues, pointing to their origin in R. B. McKerrow's influential essay, "A Suggestion Regarding Shakespeare's Manuscripts" (no. 165), which he then reprints. Several essays challenge McKerrow's hypothesis that the origins of copy for printed plays can be discriminated from the principle that irregular speech headings indicate authorial copy because copy deriving from a promptbook would have regularized speech headings: Paul Werstine, "McKerrow's 'Suggestion' and W. W. Greg" (11-16); William B. Long, "Perspectives on Provenance: The Context of Varying Speech-heads" (21-44); and Random Cloud/Randall McLeod, "What's the Bastard's Name? Random Cloud," (133-209). Many authors contribute essays on specific texts: A. R. Braunmuller examines *John*; Sidney Thomas, *Romeo*; Thomas Clayton, *Coriolanus*; Steven Urkowitz, *2 Henry VI* and *Richard III*; and Richard Proudfoot, plays from the *Apocrypha*.

V. CANON

A. Constitution of the Canon.

242. Brooke, C. F. Tucker, ed. *The Shakespeare Apocrypha*. Oxford: Clarendon Press, 1908.

Brooke discusses in his introduction the history of the attribution of plays to Shakespeare since the 1590s and lists 42 plays that he regards as doubtfully attributed. From these he isolates 13 that "have acquired a real claim to title" (xi) and that, with the addition of *More*, constitute his Apocrypha: *Arden of Faversham*; *Locrine*; *Edward III*; *Mucedorus*; *The First Part of Sir John Oldcastle*; *Thomas Lord Cromwell*; *The London Prodigal*; *The Puritan [Widow]*; *A Yorkshire Tragedy*; *The Merry Devil of Edmonton*; *Fair Em*; *Kinsmen*; *The Birth of Merlin*. The introduction includes a discussion of the printing or manuscript origin of each text; a description of its link to Shakespeare and the history of the attribution; a critical history of the play; and his own critical assessment. He pays special attention to the claims of *Edward III* and *Kinsmen*, though attributing neither to Shakespeare; he accepts the 172 lines of the insurrection scene in *More* as exhibiting "the surest indications of Shakespearean authorship" (li).

243. Erdman, David V., and Ephim G. Fogel. "Shakespeare." In *Evidence for Authorship: Essays on Problems of Attribution*, ed. David V. Erdman and Ephim G. Fogel, 432–94. Ithaca: Cornell Univ. Press, 1966.

After a series of essays on attribution that includes a reprinting of R. C. Bald, "*The Book of Sir Thomas More* and its Problems," *Shakespeare Survey* 2 (1949): 44–65, Erdman and Fogel print an "Annotated Bibliography of Selected Readings"; the Shakespeare bibliography is part of the section "English literature 1500 to 1660." They discuss ten plays: the three *Henry VI* plays together, *Titus*, *The Shrew*, *Henry VIII*, *Edward III*, *More*, *Pericles*, and *Kinsmen*. Each subject is introduced by a thorough introductory essay discussing the history of its attribution, which is followed by a chronological annotated bibliography of scholarship up to 1963.

244. Hope, Jonathan. *The Authorship of Shakespeare's Plays: A Sociolinguistic Study*. Cambridge: Cambridge Univ. Press, 1994.

Hope adapts techniques of sociolinguistics to determine questions of authorship in collaborative plays (*Henry VIII, Kinsmen, Timon, Macbeth*) and in apocryphal plays. He founds his work in the context of change in language practice in the period, and specifically on studies of relative use of auxiliary "do," of forms of relative pronouns, and (to a lesser extent) of "thou" and "you." On the basis of numerical tabulations he assigns sections of *Henry VIII* and *Kinsmen* to Shakespeare and Fletcher, concludes that the second hand in *Timon* is not identifiable, and states that the samples are too small to be significant for *Macbeth*. He suggests that *Pericles* may represent some form of collaboration between Shakespeare and Wilkins. Of the apocryphal plays he concludes that few can be associated with Shakespeare, but that *Edward III* is the best candidate for inclusion within the canon and that *Ironside* merits further investigation. Hope's method is technical, and charts and tables illustrate his argument; a final chapter, "Summary of Findings," presents his conclusions succinctly in easily accessible form.

245. Maxwell, Baldwin. *Studies in the Shakespeare Apocrypha.* New York: Columbia Univ. Press (King's Crown Press), 1956.

Maxwell is concerned with four plays that were included in the Third Folio: *Locrine, Thomas Lord Cromwell, The Puritan [Widow],* and *A Yorkshire Tragedy*. Each had previously been published in Shakespeare's lifetime; the title page of *Locrine* describes it as "Newly set foorth, ouerseene and corrected, by W. S."; those of *Thomas Lord Cromwell* and *The Puritan [Widow]* give the author as "W. S.," and that of *A Yorkshire Tragedy* attributes the play to "W. Shakespeare." Maxwell reviews initially the significance of the use of initials; he observes that no "authentic work" of Shakespeare appeared with an attribution by initials rather than by name and suggests that the use of the name may have been designed to avoid confusion with other writers with the same initials, whom he discusses; he does not attribute fraudulent motives to the printers. His discussion of individual plays seeks evidence for the identity of their real authors; only in the case of *A Yorkshire Tragedy* does he suggest that Shakespeare may have made even a minor contribution to the text, and in that instance he suggests that the ascription on the title page is either "an innocent error or a deliberate fraud."

246. Metz, G. Harold. *Sources of Four Plays Ascribed to Shakespeare.* Columbia: Univ. of Missouri Press, 1989.

Metz provides studies for *Edward III, More, Cardenio,* and *Kinsmen* modeled on Geoffrey Bullough's *Narrative and Dramatic Sources* (no. 15). In the preface he summarizes briskly the history of the formation of the canon and the debate about the apocryphal works. The introduction to each play surveys fully the scholarship concerning publication, date of composition, and authorship before the relationship to sources is addressed.

247. *Mr William Shakespear's Comedies, Histories, and Tragedies.* London 1664.

The Third Folio reprints the contents of the First and Second Folios and then adds seven plays "never before Printed in Folio": *Pericles, The London Prodigal, Thomas Lord Cromwell, Sir John Oldcastle, The Puritan Widow, A Yorkshire Tragedy,* and *Locrine.*

248. Muir, Kenneth. *Shakespeare as Collaborator.* London: Methuen, 1960.

Arguing that, because of the lack of substantial external evidence, only internal evidence can identify Shakespeare's hand in non-Folio plays, Muir examines *Edward III, Pericles,* and *Kinsmen* for "resemblances in versification, in vocabulary, in treatment of similar themes, in imagery, and the use of the same image clusters" (4). He concludes that in *Edward III* Shakespeare revised a play by another dramatist, rewriting some scenes; that in *Pericles* he again revised a play by another dramatist, very extensively in the last three acts, although he regards the extant text as a "garbled version" of Shakespeare's work; and that of *Kinsmen* Shakespeare wrote 1.1–1.4, 3.1, 5.1, and 5.4. Muir also considers the relation of Theobald's *The Double Falsehood* to Shakespeare and Fletcher's *Cardenio,* but he discerns no clear indicators to establish Shakespeare's authorship of part of *Cardenio.*

249. Schoenbaum, S. *Internal Evidence and Elizabethan Dramatic Authorship: An Essay in Literary History and Method.* Evanston, Ill.: Northwestern Univ. Press, 1966.

In the first two parts Schoenbaum presents a detailed history of studies in authorship and attribution from the seventeenth century to the time of his writing; references to the construction of the Shakespeare canon and to the practices of the disintegrators is frequent. In the third he reviews and evaluates the usefulness of various kinds of external evidence—title pages, the Stationers' Register, catalogues, etc.; he enunciates eight principles to guide investigators of authorship; and he comments on the qualities and limitations of various modes of testing (verse tests, image tests, parallel passages, and literary correspondences). An appendix makes the case for increased investigation into the nature of collaboration.

250. Taylor, Gary. "The Canon and Chronology of Shakespeare's Plays." In *William Shakespeare: A Textual Companion,* ed. Stanley Wells and Gary Taylor with John Jowett and William Montgomery, 69–144. Oxford: Clarendon Press, 1987. Repr., with corrections, New York: W. W. Norton, 1997.

In pages 69–89 of the companion volume (see no. 169) to the Oxford *Complete Works* (1986) Taylor discusses the composition of the canon in relation to the nature and value of external and internal evidence. He starts from the inclusion of works in the Folio, noting that while it may have omitted later collaborative works such as *Pericles, Cardenio,* and *Kinsmen,* it gives no indication about the possibility of collaboration in early plays; he discusses the problems concerning both plays and poems ascribed to "W. S." His discussion of internal evidence for authorship reviews and assesses its various forms: biographical evidence; palaeographical evidence; theatrical provenance; chronological evidence; vocabulary; oaths and exclamations; imagery; image clusters; verbal parallels; structural parallels; metrical evidence; linguistic evidence; stage directions; stylometry; and function words. The study of function words includes an examination of seven statistical tables that present comparative data concerning the distribution of ten function words in canonical works, in works that have been attributed to Shakespeare, and in works by other authors. It includes examinations of separate sections of plays in which collaboration is suspected (*Macbeth, Timon, Pericles*). Taylor explains the limitations of the tests, but argues that they exclude *Ironside* from possible Shakespearean authorship, while the evidence concerning *Arden of Faversham* and *Edward III* is ambiguous. In pages 109–41 Taylor presents a "sustained synthesis and assessment of evidence for authorship and chronology throughout the canon" (109), the first since E. K. Chambers in 1930 (nos. 17, 30); despite the title of the essay, he discusses both nondramatic and dramatic works. The external and internal evidence is summarized for each play and for the poems included in the Oxford edition and then for those plays and poems associated with Shakespeare's name excluded from the edition. This essay is the best introduction to the issues concerning the constitution of the canon.

251. Ule, Louis. *A Concordance to the Shakespeare Apocrypha.* 3 vols. Hildesheim, Germany: Georg Olms Verlag, 1987.

Ule presents a concordance of 13 plays: *Arden of Faversham; Edward III; The Famous Victories of Henry V; The History of Henry IV* (the Dering MS in the Folger Shakespeare Library); *Ironside; The Troublesome Reign of King John; The Second Part of the Troublesome Reign of King John; The Chronicle History of King Leir; The Tragedy of Richard III* (an anonymous play, printed in 1594); *A Shrew; Woodstock; Contention;* and *True Tragedy.* In the first two volumes each play is presented in an edited text with modernized spelling and minimal emendation; the text is followed by a word index, a ranked vocabulary-frequency list, a statistical summary of the features of the language of the play, and various frequency distributions. The third volume includes a master concordance, a frequency-ranked vocabulary, and a reverse alphabetical vocabulary for all 13 plays together. They are followed by a series of statistical tables concerning vocabulary overlap among these plays, seven plays of Marlowe, and five plays of Shakespeare: *Richard II*, *1 Henry IV*, *Henry V*, *Caesar*, and *Antony*. There are also a table of Elizabethan texts ranked by vocabulary size that includes 83 Shakespearean, apocryphal, and non-Shakespearean dramatic and nondramatic works, and a table of Shakespeare's vocabulary structure, which lists how many words he used and how many times he used each word.

See also 43, 47, 57, 140, 241, 252, 253, 254, 255, 256, 257, 258, 259, 260, 261, 262, 263, 264, 265, 266, 267.

B. Works Currently Disputed.

1. Edmund Ironside.

252. Jackson, MacD. P. "Shakespeare and 'Edmund Ironside.'" *Notes and Queries* 208 (1963): 331–32.

Jackson cautiously discusses an image cluster (see no. 121) of which the keyword is "blot" that connects *Ironside* to 13 plays and to *Venus and Adonis* and *The Rape of Lucrece*. Having noted the absence of a comparable cluster in other dramatists of the time, he nevertheless questions the validity of image clusters as internal evidence for authorship, citing a correspondence between the language of a passage in *Lear* and that of a poem by Percy Bysshe Shelley.

253. Sams, Eric, ed. *Shakespeare's Lost Play: Edmund Ironside*. London: Fourth Estate; New York: St. Martin's Press, 1985.

Sams argues vigorously in his "avowedly polemical and anything but diplomatic edition" (1) that *Ironside* is an apprentice work of Shakespeare, written around 1588. In the introduction he summarizes the basis for his conclusions and then elaborates upon them extensively in his commentary, frequently citing parallels with the early plays, especially *Titus* and the *Henry VI* plays. He pays particular attention to the occurrence in *Ironside* of numerous words recorded by OED first in Shakespeare, distinctive vocabulary and verbal habits, and image patterns and clusters; similarities in reading and learning (Ovid, Plutarch, the Bible); thematic concerns and plot details; and dramaturgical techniques.

See also nos. 244, 250, 251, 256.

2. *Edward III.*

254. Hart, Alfred. "The Vocabulary of *Edward III.*" In *Shakespeare and the Homilies*, 219–41. Melbourne: Melbourne Univ. Press in association with Oxford Univ. Press, 1934.

Hart subjects the vocabulary of *Edward III* to numerous tests, the results of which he presents in tables with commentary. He argues for Shakespeare's authorship of *Edward III* on several grounds: that, having the largest vocabulary in proportion to its length of any play of the 1590s, it has more in common with the plays of Shakespeare than those of any other playwright; that it shares common vocabulary with Shakespeare's plays but not with Marlowe's; that its vocabulary shares distinctive traits with that of Shakespeare's plays in respect to the incidence of words beginning with particular prefixes, nouns and adjectives with particular suffixes, and compound adjectives. Because these characteristic features are distributed equally throughout the play, he argues that the whole play is by Shakespeare.

255. Proudfoot, Richard. "*The Reign of King Edward III* (1596) and Shakespeare." *Proceedings of the British Academy* 71 (1985): 159–85. Published separately, London: British Academy, 1986.

In the British Academy Shakespeare lecture for 1985, Proudfoot devotes most of his attention to literary and historical criticism, but he also argues that characteristics of the play's language, especially the large vocabulary and the imagery, indicate similarities to the works of Shakespeare and to no other known playwright of the time.

256. Sams, Eric, ed. *Shakespeare's "Edward III."* New Haven: Yale Univ. Press, 1996.

After printing a text of the play, Sams summarizes the history of scholarship concerning *Edward III*, describing the kinds of uncertainty that scholars express about attributing it to Shakespeare alone, and the increasing favor with which the idea of his contribution to the text—specifically the Countess scenes—has recently been viewed. In a chapter entitled "The Case for Shakespeare," Sams presents his evidence for Shakespeare's sole authorship at length under multiple headings: he cites examples of similarities in vocabulary—the occurrence of words whose first use OED attributes to Shakespeare after the publication of *Edward III*, the distinctive use of compound words, the richness of the otherwise non-Shakespearean vocabulary, the habit of using words as different parts of speech from customary (functional shift); he cites characteristic images and image clusters, especially the density of references to flora and fauna; he notes comparable stylistic habits—in puns and wordplay, alliteration, antithesis, chiasmus, and the use of Ovid and Plutarch as sources; and numerous parallels with later-published canonical works. Suggesting that the standard of proof should be "preponderance of probability," Sams argues for single authorship by Shakespeare, and in two appendixes claims that the author of *Edward III* is identical with that of *Ironside* and with Hand D of *More*.

257. Slater, Eliot. *The Problem of Edward III: A Statistical Approach*. Cambridge: Cambridge Univ. Press, 1988.

Slater reviews the history of scholarship concerning the role of Shakespeare as possible author of or contributor to *Edward III*, and then describes the history of computer-assisted studies of style and attribution. Founding his work on Hart's studies of Shakespeare's vocabulary (no. 123) and his own prior investigations of the incidence of Shakespeare's rare words (those occurring 12 or fewer times in the canon), by which their clusterings provide evidence for probable dating, Slater determines that there is a strong correspondence between the rare-word vocabulary of Shakespeare and of *Edward III*; that although differences in vocabulary are significant for part A (1.2, 2, and 4.4) and part B of *Edward III*, they do not deny his possible authorship of both parts but could indicate that part B was written earlier. Slater concludes that the evidence is "compatible with authorship by Shakespeare at an early stage in his dramatic career" (135). Extensive appendixes provide the statistical lists and tables on which Slater bases his arguments.

See also nos. 242, 244, 246, 248, 250, 251.

3. *A Funeral Elegy*.

258. Elliott, Ward E. Y., and Robert J. Valenza. "Glass Slippers and Seven-League Boots: C-Prompted Doubts About Ascribing *A Funeral Elegy* and *A Lover's Complaint* to Shakespeare." *Shakespeare Quarterly* 48 (1997): 177–207.

On the basis of their own computer-based researches into the authorship of the Shakespeare canon, Elliott and Valenza suggest in response to Foster (nos. 261, 262) that the tests to which Foster subjected *A Funeral Elegy* should be interpreted more cautiously, and that the force of contrary evidence should be acknowledged. They argue that the majority of Foster's tests are "green light" tests that note the sharing of rare words and distinctive quirks. They argue that the validity of such tests is also limited by their propensity to produce false positives (the identification of the trait in other writers), and that the results of such tests should be treated less confidently than is Foster's practice. They stress the importance of "red light" tests also, in which the absence of a distinctive trait or anomalous word choice is seen as significant. Elliott and Valenza argue that not only *A Funeral Elegy* but *A Lover's Complaint* as well fails too many tests to be accepted as of Shakespearean authorship.

259. "Forum: *A Funeral Elegy* by W. S." *Shakespeare Studies* 25 (1997): 89–237.

The forum begins with an introduction by Leeds Barroll in which he introduces and briefly summarizes the essays. The first is a reprinting of Donald Foster's essay "*A Funeral Elegy*: W[illiam] S[hakespeare]'s 'Best-Speaking Witnesses,'" which is preceded by the edited and annotated text of the poem from that article (no. 262) (95–140). Richard Abrams ("'Exercise in This Kind': Shakespeare and the 'Funeral Elegy' for William Peter," (141–70) argues on stylistic grounds for correspondences with *Kinsmen*. Succeeding essays (with one exception) challenge the ascription to Shakespeare. In "Empirically Determining Shakespeare's Idiolect" (171–85) Ian Lancashire explores problems in the conception of the "author" and the identification of the authorial idiolect. Stanley Wells notes in "'A Funeral Elegy': Obstacles to Belief" (186–91) Foster's determiners of Shakespeare's style and presents contraindications in the form of linguistic traits in the poem uncharacteristic of Shakespeare; he raises issues concerning the relation of Foster's editing of the poem to his analysis. In "Who Wrote *A Funerall Elegie?*" (192–210) Katherine Duncan-Jones assembles the evidence of authorial self-construction in the poem to propose that the authorial voice is puritan in sympathies and so unrelated to Shakespeare's personal experience; she proposes Willam Sclater as a more likely candidate for authorship. Noting that elegies were written on command by authors not well acquainted with their subjects, Leah S. Marcus proposes in "Who Was Will Peter? Or, A Plea for Literary History" (211–28) that far more research is needed into the London and Warwickshire archives and into the Devonshire environment of William Peter. Stephen Booth reviews some of the characteristic forms that this scholarly argument takes; he concludes by acknowledging, in the context of his view that the poem is, in his title, "A Long, Dull Poem by William Shakespeare" (229–37), that Foster has been elsewhere very successful in identifying anonymous modern authors.

260. "Responses: Forum: *A Funeral Elegy* by W. S." *Shakespeare Studies* 26 (1998): 289–314.

This collection comprises responses to the essays in the "Forum" (no.

259). In "Shakespeare and the Peters in History" (291–95) Donald Foster responds to the essays of Katherine Duncan-Jones and Leah S. Marcus by presenting archival research into the Peter family and its neighbors in Devonshire; his evidence indicates that the families had no puritan connections. Ian Lancashire ("Paradigms of Authorship," 296–301) defends stylometrics against the unscientific skepticism of Wells, Duncan-Jones, Marcus, and Booth; he explains how stylometrics aims to detect the substylistic, the marks of the individual verbal unconscious, rather than the conscious stylistic choice. In "Exit Sclater" (302–14) Richard Abrams attacks the grounds of Duncan-Jones's identification of Sclater as the possible author.

261. Foster, Donald W. *Elegy By W. S.: A Study in Attribution.* Newark: Univ. of Delaware Press, 1989.

Foster presents a facsimile reproduction and an edited text of *A Funerall Elegye* (1612) by "W. S." He then submits the poem to an exhaustive study in which he documents the various qualities of the poem that make its attribution to Shakespeare plausible. He uses as a basis for comparisons not just Shakespeare's canonical texts but a large database of works of other poets, especially elegists of the time and known authors with similar initials. He treats various kinds of internal evidence: similarities of expression in the dedication, of prosody, of diction, of habits of versification, of syntax and accidence, and of spelling. He presents statistical studies of vocabulary use and also examples of thematic and verbal affinity (parallel passages). He reviews critically the internal biographical evidence and the external evidence, and then makes clear the extent of the contrary evidence. The candidacy of William Strachey for the honor of authorship is subjected to a similar examination. In a final chapter in which he examines the theory and practice of attribution, Foster does not claim that he has proved Shakespeare's authorship of the poem, but submits the evidence for others' consideration, confessing, however, that it "looks to [him] like the work of William Shakespeare" (243).

262. Foster, Donald W. "*A Funeral Elegy*: W[illiam] S[hakespeare]'s 'Best-Speaking Witnesses.'" *PMLA* 111 (1996): 1080–1105. Repr. in no. 259.

Foster presents evidence that supplements his book on *A Funeral Elegy* (no. 261). Using data derived from tests on his SHAXICON database, he discusses distinctive word forms, the use of "who" with inanimate nouns, and the incidence of hendiadys. He notes connections between the poem and Shakespeare's canonical rare word vocabulary; he shows particular correspondences in the rare word vocabulary of *A Funeral Elegy* and *Henry*

VIII. He concludes his argument by reviewing and rejecting the claims to authorship of the poem of writers proposed by other critics. An edited and annotated edition of the poem follows the essay.

See also no. 47.

4. *The Book of Sir Thomas More*.

263. Blayney, Peter W. M. "*The Booke of Sir Thomas Moore* Re-Examined." *Studies in Philology* 69 (1972): 167-91.

Blayney describes the arrangement of the *More* manuscript and then from an analysis of its features proposes a reconstruction of the process of its origins. He suggests that there were two stages of revision of the play. He hypothesizes that Munday's original draft of the work of Chettle, Heywood, and himself was returned by Edmund Tilney, the Master of the Revels, for changes; that it was at that stage when others were rewriting also that Shakespeare penned the Hand D passage; that when the manuscript was resubmitted to Tilney he returned it with the instructions for changes that survive in the manuscript; that further revisions were made, but that at some time afterwards the project was abandoned with the manuscript in a confused state. Blayney admits that his narrative is "hypothesis piled upon hypothesis" (170), but argues that it takes account of the material. On the basis of echoes between language in the play, especially of the Hand D passage, and Chettle's *Kind-Harts Dreame* (1592), he dates Shakespeare's contribution to the play to October/ November 1592. He then concludes with a proposed timetable of the events of the history of the play from early 1592 to early 1593.

264. Howard-Hill, T. H., ed. *Shakespeare and "Sir Thomas More": Essays on the play and its Shakespearian interest.* Cambridge: Cambridge Univ. Press, 1989.

Howard-Hill presents an introduction to essays by eight scholars on various aspects of *More*; not all address the question of Shakespearean authorship directly. G. Harold Metz ("'Voyce and credyt': the scholars and *Sir Thomas More*," 11-44) provides a description of the history of the play's scholarship. In "*The Book of Sir Thomas More*: dates and acting companies" (57-76), Scott McMillin summarizes much of the argument of his book (no. 266) but without repeating his identification of Hand C with Hand D. Gary Taylor reviews the evidence for the association of the play with Henslowe and for the dates of its origination and its revision in "The date and auspices of the additions to *Sir Thomas More*" (101-29). He proposes that, while the play may originate with Henslowe between 1592 and 1595, the revisions, including the Hand D material, were made in 1603-4, and could have been made under the auspices of the King's Men. In "Webster or Shakespeare? Style, idiom, vocabulary, and spelling in the additions to *Sir Thomas More*" (151-70), Charles Forker, using concordances of both authors, argues for Shakespeare rather than Webster as Hand D on the basis of internal evidence. John W. Velz reviews verbal, thematic, and dramaturgical analogues elsewhere in the Shakespearean canon to give cautious support to the Shakespearean identity of Hand D ("*Sir Thomas More* and the Shakespeare canon: two approaches" [171-95]).

265. Kinney, Arthur F. "Text, Context, and Authorship of *The Booke of Sir Thomas Moore*." In *Pilgrimage for Love: Essays in Early Modern Literature in Honor of Josephine A. Roberts,* ed. Sigrid King, 133-60. Tempe, Ariz.: Arizona Center for Medieval and Renaissance Studies, 1999.

Kinney argues against the identification of Shakespeare as the author of the Hand D passage. He initially reviews positively earlier challenges to the identification of the handwriting and spelling as distinctively Shakespeare's and to vocabulary evidence cited as related to Shakespearean verbal habits. He then argues that other features of the writing—its language and rhetoric, but particularly the sympathetic portrayal of the rebels' cause—do not correspond to the characteristics of canonical Shakespearean texts, and on this basis denies authorship. See also Carol A. Chillington, "Playwrights at Work: Henslowe's, Not Shakespeare's, *Book of Sir Thomas More*," *English Literary Renaissance* 10 (1980): 439-79, who argues that Hand D is that of John Webster.

266. McMillin, Scott. *The Elizabethan Theatre and "The Book of Sir Thomas More."* Ithaca and London: Cornell Univ. Press, 1987.

McMillin's examination of the manuscript play argues that it is a promptbook used for the preparation of actors' parts prior to the preparation of the final promptbook, and that in its extant condition it is not fragmentary and incoherent but an actable play whose staging would indicate a "sophisticated dramaturgy" (105). He suggests that it was originally written for the Lord Strange's Men at the Rose Playhouse, and that it was revised about 1603 for the Lord Admiral's Men. He proposes that Hand D was that not of one of the later revisers but of one of the original collaborators. He neither endorses nor denies the identification of Hand D as Shakespeare's, but he proposes that Hand D and Hand C are identical.

267. Pollard, A. W., ed. *Shakespeare's Hand in The Play of "Sir Thomas*

More." Shakespeare Problems 2. Cambridge: Cambridge Univ. Press, 1923.

In an introductory essay (1–40) Pollard describes the history of the identification of Hand D as that of Shakespeare and reviews the arguments of the succeeding articles. W. W. Greg (41–56) describes the hands of the manuscript, but leaves the discussion of Hand D to Sir Edward Maunde Thompson, who elaborates (57–112) on his argument in *Shakespeare's Handwriting* (Oxford: Clarendon Press, 1916). By a detailed examination of letter forms he suggests that there are significant points of resemblance between the six signatures and Hand D, and suggests that the signatures, which all date from the last three years of Shakespeare's life, indicate deterioration in handwriting as a result of illness. In "Bibliographical Links between the Three Pages and the Good Quartos" (113–41), J. Dover Wilson argues that misprints and distinctive spellings found in Good Quartos are consonant with printing from manuscript copy such as the three pages. R. W. Chambers (142–87) discusses similarities in the expression of ideas between the three pages and other passages in Shakespeare's plays, especially *Troilus* and *Coriolanus*. A text edited by W. W. Greg of the "Ill May Day" scenes from the play (189–227) is included, as well as a "Special Transcript of the Three Pages," also prepared by W. W. Greg (228–[43]). See also W. W. Greg, "Shakespeare's Hand Once More" in *Collected Papers* (no. 153), where he expresses doubt whether the palaeographic evidence alone constitutes proof of Shakespeare's authorship of the three pages of *More* and argues that belief in the identification must proceed from the "convergence of a number of independent lines of argument—palaeographic, orthographic, linguistic, stylistic, psychological—and not on any one alone" (200).

See also nos. 34, 60, 92, 107, 132, 153, 242, 243, 246.

INDEX I: AUTHORS AND EDITORS (FOR SECTIONS II, III, IV, AND V)

Citations are to item number. Please note that authors may also appear in the subject index.

Abbott, E. A., 97
Abrams, Richard, 259, 260
Alden, Raymond Macdonald, 198
Alexander, Nigel, 67
Alexander, Peter, 223
Allen, Michael J. B., 135
Andrews, John F., 68, 120
Armstrong, Edward A., 121
Aubrey, John, 28

Baker, Oliver, 41
Bald, R. C., 243
Baldwin, T. W., 102
Banks, Carol, 237a
Barber, Charles, 69
Barish, Jonas A., 116
Barroll, Leeds, 259
Bartlett, Henrietta C., 139, 140
Bawcutt, N. W., 67
Bearman, Robert, 42
Bentley, Gerald Eades, 43
Berger, Thomas L., 137, 235, 236
Bergeron, David M., 205
Bevington, David, 197
Black, Matthew W., 206
Blake, N[orman] F., 70, 71, 97
Bland, Mark, 235
Blayney, Peter W. M., 136, 149, 150, 233, 263
Bolton, W. F., 72
Booth, Stephen, 138, 259

Bowers, Fredson, 207
Bracy, William, 171
Braunmuller, A. R., 236, 241
Brinkworth, E. R. C, 44
Brock, Susan, 50
Brook, G. L., 73
Brooke, C. F. Tucker, 29, 242
Brooks, Douglas, 220
Burkhart, Robert E., 172
Burness, Edwina, 79, 99, 106, 109, 110, 111, 115, 125, 127
Burnett, Mark Thornton, 67
Burton, Dolores M., 98

Caie, Graham D., 237a
Capell, Edward, 143
Cercignani, Fausto, 80
Chambers, E. K. (Sir Edmund), 30, 37, 45, 151, 187
Chambers, R. W., 267
Charney, Maurice, 184
Chillington, Carol A., 265
Clark, William George, 144
Clayton, Thomas, 194, 241
Clegg, Cyndia Susan, 235
Clemen, Wolfgang, 129
Cloud, Random, *see* McLeod, Randall
Coghill, Nevill, 188
Colman, E. A. M., 88
Colaianni, Louis, 81
Condell, Henry, 145

Cox, Jane, 62
Cox, John D, 233
Craig, Hardin, 174
Crane, Milton, 117
Cusack, Bridget, 99

Davidson, Adele, 175
De Grazia, Margreta, 208, 209, 210, 238
Dent, R. W., 82
Dessen, Alan C., 152, 217
Dick, Oliver Lawson, 28
Digges, L[eonard], 32
Dillon, Janette, 211
Dobson, E. J., 83
Donawerth, Jane, 114
Doran, Madeleine, 197
Dowden, Edward, 30
Duncan-Jones, Katherine, 259
Duthie, George Ian, 176
Dutton, Richard, 67, 239

Eagleson, Robert D., 86
Eccles, Mark, 46
Edelman, Charles, 84
Elam, Keir, 240
Elliott, Ward E. Y., 258
Elton, W. R., 218
Empson, William, 122
Erdman, David V., 243
Evans, N. E., 61, 63
Ewbank, Inga-Stina, 100

Fabian, Bernhard, 229
Findlay, Alison, 67
Foakes, R. A., 67, 212
Fogel, Ephim G., 243
Forker, Charles, 264
Foster, Donald W., 47, 259, 260, 261, 262
Francis, Frank C., 170
Fripp, Edgar I., 36
Furnivall, F. J., 37

Gaines, Barry, 137

Gardner, Helen, 94, 170
Gaskell, Philip, 131
Glover, John, 144
Goldberg, Jonathan, 189, 237, 238
Goldring, Beth, 194
Gordon, D. J., 67
Graham-White, Anthony, 199
Gray, Joseph William, 33
Greg, W. W., 137, 153, 154, 155, 156, 177, 178, 197, 213, 214, 215, 267

Habicht, Werner, 52, 184
Halio, Jay L., 197
Halliday, M. A. K., 105
Hamer, Douglas, 48
Hammond, Antony, 237
Hart, Alfred, 123, 157, 158, 179, 254
Heminge, John, 145
Herford, C. H., 146
Hill, W. Speed, 226, 234
Hinman, Charlton, 136, 137, 159
Holderness, Graham, 216, 237a, 240
Honan, Park, 49
Honigmann, E. A. J., 50, 51, 52, 67, 190, 191, 217
Hope, Jonathan, 74, 244
Houston, John Porter, 101
Howard-Hill, T. H., 132, 264
Hulme, Hilda M., 124, 125
Hussey, S. S., 75

Immroth, John Philip, 164
Ingleby, C. M., 37
Ioppolo, Grace, 192
Irace, Kathleen O., 180

Jackson, MacD[onald] P., 134, 160, 194, 200, 252
Jenkins, Harold, 67
Jones, Jeanne E., 53
Jonson, Ben, 32, 146
Jorgensen, Paul, 122
Joseph, Sister Miriam, C.S.C., 102
Jowett, John, 134, 166, 169, 218, 250

INDEX I: AUTHORS AND EDITORS

Kastan, David Scott, 74, 108, 120, 228, 233, 234, 235, 236, 238, 240
Keen, Alan, 54
Keilen, Sean, 182, 209, 225, 227, 234, 237, 238
Kerrigan, John, 194
Kidnie, Margaret Jane, 231
King, Sigrid, 226, 265
Kinney, Arthur F., 265
Kökeritz, Helge, 85

Lancashire, Ian, 259, 260
Lander, Jesse M., 235
Lanham, Richard A., 103
Lee, [Sir] Sidney, 34, 141, 161
Leech, Clifford, 67, 116
Levenson, Jill L., 137
Loewenstein, Joseph F., 236
Long, William B., 162, 163, 235, 241
Longworth, Clara, Countess of Chambrun, 51
Loughrey, Bryan, 216, 240
Lubbock, Roger, 54

Macdonald, Màiri, 55
Magnoni, Stefania, 240
Magnusson, Lynne, 104
Maguire, Laurie E., 181, 235, 236, 237a
Mahood, M. M., 126
Malone, Edmond, 35, 147
Marcus, Leah S., 219, 237a, 259
Margeson, J. M. R., 116
Massai, Sonia, 240
Masten, Jeffrey, 220, 233
Maxwell, Baldwin, 245
Maxwell, J. C., 153, 215
McGann, Jerome J., 190
McIntosh, Angus, 105
McJannet, Linda, 152
McKenzie, D. F., 201, 202, 221
McKerrow, R[onald]. B., 131, 164, 165, 222, 223, 241
McLeod, Randall, 173, 194, 224, 225, 237, 238, 241

McManaway, James G., 134
McMillin, Scott, 182, 238, 264, 266
McMullan, Gordon, 240
Melchiori, Giorgio, 240
Merchant, W. Moelwyn, 67
Metz, G. Harold, 246, 264
Miller, Stephen Roy, 137, 236
Milward, Peter, 51
M Leod, Randall, see McLeod, Randall
Montgomery, William, 137, 169, 250
Mowat, Barbara A., 226, 236, 239
Mucciolo, John M., 218
Muir, Kenneth, 109, 115, 135, 248
Mulholland, Joan, 106
Munro, John, 37
Murphy, Andrew, 216, 237a

Neidig, William, 155
Ness, F. W., 118
Nosworthy, J. M., 193

Onions, C. T., 86
Orgel, Stephen, 182, 209, 225, 227, 228, 234, 237, 238

Palmer, D. J., 52, 184
Parker, R. B., 66, 239
Partridge, A. C., 76, 77, 107
Partridge, Eric, 87
Pendry, E. D., 67
Pitcher, John, 234
Platt, Peter G., 108
Pollard, Alfred W., 139, 155, 183, 267
Porter, Stanley E., 237a
Potter, Lois, 67, 240
Price, Diana, 47
Pringle, Roger, 52, 184
Proudfoot, Richard, 134, 241, 255

Quirk, Randolph, 109

Rasmussen, Eric, 134, 233
Replogle, Carol, 127
Rogers, Joyce, 56
Ronberg, Gert, 78

Rowe, Nicholas, 38, 148
Rubinstein, Frankie, 88

Salgādo, Gāmini, 67
Salmon, Vivian, 79, 99, 106, 109, 110, 111, 112, 115, 125, 127, 203
Sams, Eric, 57, 253, 256
Sanders, Norman, 67
Sarrazin, Gregor, 89
Savage, Richard, 36
Schmidt, Alexander, 89
Schoenbaum, S., 58, 59, 60, 64, 109, 115, 249
Scragg, Leah, 67
Serpieri, Alessandro, 240
Shaaber, Matthias A., 206
Shady, Raymond C., 224
Shand, G. B., 224
Shapiro, I. A., 67
Shirley, Frances Ann, 128
Simpson, Evelyn, 146
Simpson, Percy, 146, 204
Sipe, Dorothy, 120
Skura, Meredith, 239
Slater, Eliot, 257
Smart, John Semple, 39
Smith, Bruce R., 205
Smith, Charles G., 90
Smith, Emma, 237a
Smith, Lucy Toulmin, 37
Smithers, G. V., 113
Sokol, B. J., 91
Sokol, Mary, 91
Spevack, Marvin, 68, 92, 93
Spurgeon, Caroline, 129
Stallybrass, Peter, 209, 228, 237a, 238
Steppat, Michael, 237A

Tarlinskaja, Marina, 120
Taylor, Gary, 112, 166, 169, 194, 195, 197, 214, 230, 237, 237a, 238, 250, 264
Taylor, Neil, 240

Tetzeli von Rosador, Kurt, 229
Thomas, David, 62, 63
Thomas, Sidney, 241
Thompson, Ann, 240
Thompson, Sir Edward Maunde, 267
Thomson, Leslie, 152
Tilley, Morris Palmer, 94
Trousdale, Marion, 114, 196, 229

Ule, Louis, 251
Urkowitz, Steven, 184, 194, 197, 241

Valenza, Robert J., 258
Velz, John W., 264
Vickers, Brian, 68, 115, 119

Wadsworth, Frank, 65
Walker, Alice, 167
Wallace, Charles William, 40
Walton, J. K., 134, 168
Warren, Michael [J.], 194, 197
Warren, Roger, 194
Wells, Henry W., 116
Wells, Stanley, 66, 67, 87, 100, 112, 160, 169, 194, 230, 231, 240, 250, 259
Werstine, Paul, 185, 186, 194, 232, 233, 234, 236, 241
West, Anthony James, 142
Whiter, Walter, 130
Wiggins, Martin, 67
Williams, George Walton, 133, 134, 241
Williams, Gordon, 95, 96
Wilson, F. P., 94, 170
Wilson, J. Dover, 267
Wilson, Richard, 51
Woudhuysen, H. R., 134
Wright, George T., 68, 120
Wright, William Aldis, 144

Zimmerman, Susan, 234
Zitner, S. P., 66, 239

INDEX II: SUBJECTS
(FOR SECTIONS II, III, IV, AND V)

Citations are to item number. Please note that authors may also appear in the subject index.

abridgment, 151, 157, 161, 171, 172, 174, 177, 178, 180, 182, 186, 187, 197. *See also* adaptation, performance texts, revision
accent, accentuation, *see* stress
accidence, *see* grammar
accidentals, 215
acting versions, *see* performance texts
act-intervals, 166
actors, 154, 171, 181, 182, 186
actors' names, 164, 170, 182
act-scene division, 143, 148, 161, 166
Adam (*As You Like It*), 47
adaptation, 151, 171, 180, 186
adapter, 177, 236
adapter-reviser, 171
Albany (*King Lear*), 197
Alexander, Peter, 184
Alleyn, Edward, 178
allusions to Shakespeare, 29, 30, 37, 140
alphabets, 70, 81, 112
anti-Stratfordism, 39, 64, 65
Apocrypha, 43, 132, 140, 148, 169, 183, 241, 242, 243, 244, 245, 246, 247, 248, 249, 250, 251. *See also* apocryphal and attributed works
apocryphal and attributed works
—*Arden of Faversham*, 242, 250, 251

—*Birth of Merlin*, 242
—*Cardenio*, 246, 248, 250
—*Chronicle History of King Leir*, 251
—*Edmund Ironside*, 244, 250, 251, 252, 253, 256
—*Edward III*, 242, 243, 244, 246, 248, 250, 251, 254, 255, 256, 257
—*Fair Em*, 57, 242
—*Famous Victories of Henry the Fifth*, 116, 251
—*Funeral Elegy*, 47, 258, 259, 260, 261, 262
—*History of Henry IV* (Dering MS), 251
—*Locrine*, 57, 242, 245, 247
—*London Prodigal*, 242, 247
—*Merry Devil of Edmonton*, 242
—*Mucedorus*, 242
—*Puritan Widow*, 242, 245, 247
—*Second Part of the Troublesome Reign of King John*, 251
—*Sir John Oldcastle*, 242, 247
—*Sir Thomas More*, 34, 60, 92, 107, 132, 153, 205, 232, 242, 243, 246, 256, 263, 264, 265, 266, 267
—*Taming of a Shrew*, 57, 92, 137, 181, 182, 219, 236, 251
—*Thomas Lord Cromwell*, 183, 242, 245, 247

—*Tragedy of Richard III*, 251
—*Troublesome Reign of King John*, 57, 92, 251
—Ur-*Hamlet*, 57, 237a
—"Verses on John Combe," 28, 35, 38
—*Willobie His Avisa*, 57
—*Woodstock*, 162, 251
—*Yorkshire Tragedy*, 242, 245, 247
apparatus, 210, 218
Archer, Sir Simon, 55
Arden family (Shakespeare's mother), 38, 46
Arden of Faversham, see apocryphal and attributed works
Arden Shakespeare, 173
arguments, 225
Aristotle, 108
"aside," 217
association of ideas, see image clusters
attribution, 141, 242, 243, 249, 250, 255, 256, 257, 259, 261
Aubrey, John, 51
authenticity, 210, 211, 227, 245
authentic text, 147, 179, 189, 211, 227. See also original text
author-adapter, 172
authorial drafts, 156, 161, 164, 165, 166, 179, 183, 189, 226, 236, 241
author, 161, 163, 186, 191, 248
—absence of, 189, 232, 237a
—authorial punctuation, 198, 237
—collaborative authorship, 160, 220, 228, 233, 240, 244, 248, 250, 263
—concept of, 196, 208, 209, 210, 211, 212, 216, 218, 220, 226, 228, 233, 234, 236, 237a, 238, 240
—construction of, 210
—determination of, 242, 244, 245, 246, 249, 250, 252, 253, 254, 255, 256, 257, 258, 259, 260, 261, 262, 264, 265, 267
—multiple authorship, 151, 161, 187, 191, 248
—as reviser, 57, 157, 187, 188, 190, 191, 192, 193, 194, 195, 197. See also abridgment, attribution, disintegration, revision
auxiliary "do," 74, 99, 109, 110, 244

Bacon, Sir Francis, 39, 65, 129
Bad Quartos, see quartos
Baker, Oliver, 51
Bale, John, 192
bawdy, 86, 87, 88, 89, 95, 96
BBC Shakespeare Series, 181
Bearman, Robert, 66
Beaumont, Francis, 220
Beaumont[, Francis] and Fletcher [, John], 117, 220
Beaumont, Joseph, *Psyche*, 202
Belott-Mountjoy suit, 40, 60, 62
Bentley, Gerald Eades, 228
Betterton, Thomas, 38
Bible, 237a, 253
Birth of Merlin, see apocryphal and attributed works
Blackfriars Gate-House, 50, 60
Blackfriars Playhouse, 40
Blake, N[orman] F., 97
blank verse, 68, 76, 101, 120
Blayney, Peter W. M., 159, 183
Blount, Edward, 136
Bodleian Library, 135
bookbinding, 131, 133, 149
bookholder/book-keeper, 163, 233
book illustration, 131
book of the play, see promptbooks
booksellers, 233
book trade, 131, 235
Booth, Stephen, 260
borrowings, see loan words
Bowers, Fredson, 221, 232
box rules, 159
Brabantio (*Othello*), 47
British Library, 135
Bullough, Geoffrey, *Narrative and Dramatic Sources*, 246
Burbage, Richard, 50

INDEX II: SUBJECTS

Busby, John, 177

Cambridge Shakespeare, 207
Cambridge University Press, 202, 221
canon, constitution of the, 30, 160, 169, 187, 218, 246, 249, 250, 258, 261, 264, 265
Capell, Edward, 223
Cardenio, see apocryphal and attributed works
casting off copy, 160
castration, see bawdy
cast, reduced, 171, 172, 178, 182
catalogues, 249
Catholicism, 39, 41, 44, 51, 54, 57
Celia (*As You Like It*), 105
censorship, 151, 169, 235
census, of quartos, 139, 140; of folios, 140, 141, 142
Cercignani, Fausto, 85
Chambers, E. K., 30, 34, 45, 48, 51, 54, 162, 163, 191, 197, 250
change in language practice, 244
Chapman, George, 129
characters, distinctive speech of, 68, 75, 76, 98, 99, 101, 104, 105, 106, 108, 114, 116, 117, 119, 122, 126, 127, 128, 129
Chaucer, Geoffrey, 120, 239
Chettle, Henry, *Kind-Hart's Dreame*, 263
Chronicle History of King Leir, see apocryphal and attributed works
chronology (of works), 29, 30, 159, 169, 210, 250
Church Court of Stratford-upon-Avon, 44
Cicero, 108
Ciceronian style, 75
Clapham, Henoch, 203
Clark, William George, 207
Coghill, Nevill, 190
coining, see word formation
collaboration, 57, 160, 220, 227, 228, 233, 239, 240, 244, 248, 249, 250, 263, 264, 265, 266, 267
collations, 169, 206, 222
Collier, John Payne, 60
colloquial language, 69, 75, 76, 79, 101, 104, 107, 110, 124, 125
Colman, E. A. M., 87, 88
Combe, John, 28, 35, 38
Combe, Thomas, the Elder, 34
Combe, William, 55
composition (printing), 131, 133, 156, 190, 199, 224
compositors, 107, 112, 136, 149, 150, 156, 159, 160, 167, 169, 190, 198, 200, 201, 202, 203, 204, 207, 224; Compositor A, 156, 167; Compositor B, 156, 167, 203; Eld A, 200; Eld B, 200
concordances, 92, 93, 225, 251, 264
Condell, Henry, 50, 136, 183, 193
conflation, 194, 197, 225
continuous copy, 187
contracted forms, 230
copia, 75
"coppied . . . by . . . eare," 186
copy, printers', 133, 136, 151, 153, 156, 159, 161, 164, 166, 167, 168, 169, 170, 193, 201, 207, 213, 214, 226, 232, 241
copy-text, 92, 153, 213, 215, 222, 232
copyright, 149, 156, 159, 183, 210, 236
Cordelia (*King Lear*), 192
Corin (*As You Like It*), 47
correspondence, literary, 249
corruption, 157, 171, 172, 184, 190, 191, 197
Cottom, John, 51
Cox, Jane, 56
critical edition, 207
cruxes, 124, 214
Culman, Leonard, *Sententiae Pueriles*, 90

De Grazia, Margreta, 216, 239

Dekker, Thomas, 129, 204
Dering MS, 251
"derivative" texts, also "derived" texts, 213, 222
devices, printers', *see* ornaments
Devonshire, 259, 260
dialect, 69, 70, 73, 80, 89, 112, 124, 230
dialogue, 104, 125, 225
dictionaries, 69, 71, 78, 81, 82, 83, 84, 85, 86, 87, 88, 89, 91, 93, 94, 95, 96, 124, 125, 152, 253
diplomatic editions, 240
discourse analysis, 104
disintegration, 151, 187, 191, 249
disputed works, *see* apocryphal and attributed works
Donne, John, 120
Doubtful Quartos, *see* quartos
dramatis personae, 148, 161, 225
Duncan-Jones, Katherine, 260
Dyer, Sir Edward, 65

eclecticism, 191, 223
Edgar (*King Lear*), 197
editing—theory and practice before 1900, 143, 144, 147, 148, 170, 206, 210, 223
—theory and practice since 1900, 153, 166, 169, 170, 173, 191, 197, 201, 204, 207, 208, 209, 211, 212, 213, 214, 215, 216, 217, 218, 219, 222, 224, 225, 227, 229, 230, 231, 232, 234, 236, 237, 237a, 238, 240, 241. *See also* author, copy-text, electronic editions, emendation, instability, materiality, material texts, modernization, multiple text works, multiple version editions, New Bibliography, textual criticism and theory, unediting
Edmund Ironside, *see* apocryphal and attributed works
Edward III, *see* apocryphal and attributed works
Eld A, *see* compositors
Eld B, *see* compositors
electronic editions, 209, 218, 234, 237a
elegies, 259, 261
emendation, 124, 130, 143, 144, 169, 214, 215, 217, 218, 226, 231, 238, 251
Erasmus, 114
euphemisms, 87
Euphuistic style, 75
evidence, external, 169, 210, 243, 248, 249, 250, 261
evidence, internal, 169, 210, 243, 248, 249, 250, 252, 261, 264, 267
expurgation, 166
external evidence, *see* evidence, external

facsimiles, 30, 59, 60, 61, 79, 135, 136, 137, 138, 141, 154, 161, 225, 234, 238, 261
fair copy, 164, 165, 207, 222
Fair Em, *see* apocryphal and attributed works
Falstaff (*1 Henry IV*, *2 Henry IV*, *Merry Wives*), 117; (*1 Henry IV*), 236
Famous Victories of Henry the Fifth, *see* apocryphal and attributed works
figurative language, 68, 70, 71, 95, 97, 100, 115, 119, 121, 129
first draft, 171, 180, 231
first/second thoughts, 191
Fleay, F. G., 187
Fletcher, John, 220, 244, 248
Folger Shakespeare Library, 135, 136, 149, 251
Folio, Ben Jonson's, 220
Folio, First, 43, 133, 135, 136, 143, 144, 145, 147, 149, 151, 153, 156, 157, 160, 161, 170, 183, 206, 213, 220, 222, 223, 237a, 238, 239, 247, 250
—census of, 140, 141, 142

INDEX II: SUBJECTS

—comparison with quarto texts, 175, 177, 182, 188, 191, 192, 193, 194, 195, 197, 219, 225
—in concordance, 92
—copy for, 136, 143, 144, 145, 147, 149, 151, 156, 159, 160, 167, 168, 169, 170, 183
—economics of publication, 136, 149, 159
—facsimiles, 136
—printing of, 136, 149, 151, 156, 159, 160, 183
—proofreading, 136, 149, 156, 159, 160, 183
—punctuation of, 70, 107, 198, 204
—spelling of, 107
—swearing in, 128, 166. See also performance texts, revision, Shakespeare, William (individual works)
Folio, Second, 140, 161, 183, 206, 223, 235, 247
Folio, Third, 133, 140, 148, 161, 183, 206, 223, 235, 245, 247
Folio, Fourth, 140, 148, 161, 183, 206, 223, 235
Ford, John, 117
foreign languages, 28, 57, 69, 74, 75, 83, 85, 89, 90, 95, 98, 112, 124, 125
forgeries, 30, 60, 62
Forman, Simon, *Book of Plays*, 60, 237
Foster, Donald, 258, 259
foul papers, 136, 150, 156, 160, 167, 168, 169, 186, 197, 207, 213, 232, 233
function words, 250
functional shift, 70, 74, 97, 100, 111, 256
Funeral Elegy, see apocryphal and attributed works
Furnivall, F. J., 31

Gardener (*Richard II*), 47
Gascoigne, George, *Supposes*, 116
Gaunt (*Richard II*), 47

generic editions, 234
Ghost (*Hamlet*), 47
Globe Playhouse, 40, 161, 188
Globe Shakespeare, 144
glossaries, *see* dictionaries
Goldberg, Jonathan, 216
Good Quartos, *see* quartos
grammar, 69, 70, 71, 73, 74, 75, 76, 77, 79, 83, 89, 97, 98, 102, 106, 109, 111, 152, 261
grammar books, 69, 71, 83, 97, 199
Great Vowel Shift, 74
"green light" tests, 258
Greene, Robert, 51, 52; *Orlando Furioso*, 154, 178
greeting, modes of, 99
Greg, W. W., 162, 163, 170, 181, 184, 185, 229, 232, 233, 236, 241

Hall, Edward, *Chronicles*, 54
Hall, John, 52, 55
Hamlet (*Hamlet*), 117
Hand C, 264, 266
Hand D, 34, 60, 92, 153, 205, 232, 256, 263, 264, 265, 266, 267
handwriting, Elizabethan, 131; Shakespeare's 34, 60, 62, 265. *See also* Hand C, Hand D
Hart, Alfred, 184, 257
Hart, William, 50
Harvard Concordance to Shakespeare, 92, 225
Hathaway, Anne, *see* Shakespeare, Anne Hathaway family (Shakespeare's wife), 38, 46
headlines, 159
Heminge (also Heminges), John, 50, 136, 183, 193
Henry E. Huntington Library, 135
Henslowe, Philip, 264, 265
Henslowe's Diary, 187
Hesketh, Sir Thomas, 41, 45, 48
Hesketh, Thomas (of Gray's Inn), 41, 48

INDEX II: SUBJECTS

heterosexuality, language of, *see* bawdy
Heywood, John, 125
Heywood, Thomas, 186, 263
Hiccox, Lewis, 53
Highways Bill, 42
Hinman, Charlton B., 136, 221
History of Henry IV (Dering MS), *see* apocryphal and attributed works
Hoghton, Alexander, of Lea, 41, 45, 48, 51, 54, 58, 59
Holderness, Graham, 211
Homer, 239
homosexuality, language of, *see* bawdy
Honigmann, E.A.J., 66, 228
Host (*Merry Wives*), 177
hypertext editions, 234, 237a. *See also* electronic editions

iconicity, 225
ideal text, 208, 211, 213, 219, 222, 237a
idiolect, 73, 75, 93, 259
idiom, 124, 125, 264
image clusters, 68, 121, 130, 239, 248, 250, 252, 253, 256
imagery, 68, 70, 87, 95, 97, 98, 119, 129, 248, 250, 253, 255, 256
image tests, 249
imposition, 131, 133
"incarnational" text, 208
ink, 133
initials, *see* W. S.
innovations in language, Shakespearean, 68, 73, 74, 79, 99, 100, 102, 109. *See also* neologisms, vocabulary, word formation
Inns of Court, 188
instability, 191, 209, 212, 218, 226, 227, 228, 229, 234, 237
intention, 212
interpolation, 166
Ireland, William Henry, 60

Jaggard, Isaac, 136, 149, 156, 159
Jaggard, William, 136, 149, 156, 159, 183, 193, 201
Jenkins, Harold, 184
Johnson, Samuel, 35, 223
Jones, Jeanne E., 66
Jonson, Ben, 28, 38, 116, 117, 129, 157, 158, 192, 204, 220

King (*All's Well, 1 Henry IV*), 47
Keats, John, "On Sitting Down to [Read] King Lear Once Again," 225
King James Bible, 237a
King's Men, 61, 264
Kökeritz, Helge, 80, 81
Kyd, Thomas, 117

Lancashire, 45, 51, 54, 57. *See also* Hoghton, Alexander, of Lea
language of Shakespeare's time, 68, 69, 70, 71, 73, 74, 75, 79, 97, 98, 99, 100, 104, 108, 109, 110, 112, 124, 125, 127
Lee, Sir Sidney, 139, 142, 156, 166, 183, 233
legal language, 91
length of performances, 158
length of plays, 123, 157, 158, 239
letters patent, 61
lexicons, *see* dictionaries
licensing, for performance, 187; for publication, 164, 233, 235
lineation of verse, 143
Livy, 239
loan words, 69, 70, 74, 75, 89
Locrine, see apocryphal and attributed works
logic, 102, 116
London Prodigal, see apocryphal and attributed works
Lord Admiral's Men, 266
Lord Chamberlain, 155
Lord Chamberlain's Men, 61
Lord Strange's Men, 45, 51, 266

INDEX II: SUBJECTS

Loughrey, Bryan, 211
Lydgate, John, 120
Lyly, John, 116

Macdonald, Màiri, 66
Malone, Edmond, 170, 210
manuscripts, 33, 59, 95, 107, 112, 124, 146, 147, 151, 154, 162, 165, 166, 167, 168, 170, 175, 179, 186, 199, 200, 203, 208, 213, 215, 226, 233, 235, 236, 237, 242, 251, 263, 264, 265, 266, 267
Marcus, Leah S., 237a, 260
Marlowe, Christopher, 65, 76, 117, 129, 204, 219, 251, 254
Marston, John, 192
Massinger, Philip, 129
Master of the Revels, 62, 187, 263
material book, 208
materiality, 212, 216, 219, 234, 236, 237
material text, 196, 209, 211, 216, 219, 225, 237, 240
McGann, Jerome J., 216
McIntosh, Angus, 106
McKenzie, D. F., 136, 159, 203
McKerrow, R[onald]. B., 131, 156, 213, 229, 232, 241
meaning, 76, 77, 78, 98, 114, 122
meaning, changes in, 69, 73, 79, 99
memorial reconstruction, 57, 160, 169, 170, 171, 172, 174, 177, 178, 179, 180, 181, 184, 185, 186, 213, 237a
Merry Devil of Edmonton, see apocryphal and attributed works
metaphor, 68, 70, 95, 97, 100, 115, 119, 121, 129
meter, 29, 30, 68, 72, 73, 76, 79, 85, 97, 99, 107, 111, 120, 230, 249, 261
metrical tables, 30
Middleton, Thomas, 117, 166, 192
military language, 84
Milton, John, 120, 219
modernization, 144, 173, 207, 209, 217, 218, 229, 230, 231, 237a, 251
modes of address, 70, 127. *See also* pronouns of address
morphology, 68, 69
mortuaries, 56
Mucedorus, see apocryphal and attributed works
multiple text works, 173, 189, 190, 191, 192, 193, 194, 195, 196, 197, 209, 212, 213, 215, 219, 225, 226, 237a, 240
multiple version editions, 234
Munday, Anthony, 263
music, 166

names, proper, 81, 85, 93, 230, 237a, 245. *See also* speech headings
nation, language and, 69, 72
neologisms, 99, 111. *See also* innovation, loan words, word formation
New Bibliography, 161, 166, 170, 181, 183, 208, 216, 218, 219, 236, 239
New Place, 35, 50, 60, 61, 62
New Textualists, 216
non-verbal sounds, 217
Norton Shakespeare, 169
number of lines, 158

oaths, 70, 128, 166, 250
occasional plays, 193
octavo, 140
OED, see *Oxford English Dictionary*
Okes, Nicholas, 150
Oldcastle (*1 Henry IV*), 236
old-spelling, 92, 225
old-spelling editions, 73, 207, 215, 218, 222, 224, 225
Ong, Walter, 205
Onions, C. T., 89, 93
order of printing, 159, 161
Orgel, Stephen, 216, 239
original text, 189, 197, 208, 209, 210, 228, 236, 237. *See also* authentic text

ornaments, printers', 150, 155, 161, 183
orthography, *see* spelling
Ovid, 253, 256
Oxford Shakespeare *Complete Works*, 96, 169, 205, 218, 230, 236, 240, 250; *Textual Companion*, 218
Oxford, Earl of, 65
Oxford English Dictionary (OED), 93, 124, 253, 256

Padua promptbooks, 237
paper, 131, 133, 155, 161
parallel passages, 249, 261
Partridge, Eric, 87, 88, 89, 96
parts, actors', 154, 178, 179, 266
Pavier quartos, *see* quartos
Pavier, Thomas, 155
Peachum, Henry, 114
Peele, George, *Battle of Alcazar*, 178
Pembroke's Men, 182
performance, 158, 188, 211, 218, 227, 228, 233, 236, 237, 237a, 239
performance, records of, 30
performance texts, 157, 158, 171, 172, 177, 178, 179, 180, 181, 182, 183, 184, 185, 188, 193, 211, 212, 227, 233, 236, 237. *See also* abridgment, adaptation, revision
perjury, 128
Peter, William, 259, 260
phonology, 68, 69, 71, 74, 78, 80, 83, 85, 111. *See also* pronunciation
piracy, 176, 183, 233
playbooks, *see* promptbooks
plots, 154, 178
Plutarch, 253, 256
politeness, politeness theory, 104, 110
Pollard, Alfred W., 139, 155, 161, 174, 177, 178, 185, 187, 233, 236
Pope, Alexander, 223
postmodernism, 218, 234
poststructuralism, 189, 216, 234
pragmatics, 72

press, structure of, 133
press-crews, 202
press-variants, 135, 136, 144, 150, 156, 159, 160, 234
presswork, 131, 133
prices (of books), 141, 149
printers' copy, *see* copy, printers'
printing house practices, 151, 183, 199, 221, 235. *See also* printing process
printing, invention of, 133
printing, machine press, 131
printing process, 43, 131, 133, 150, 151, 156, 159, 161, 169, 170, 183, 199, 202, 207, 233, 235
printing trade, 133
print runs, 136, 159
profanity, 166
promptbooks, 107, 136, 151, 154, 156, 160, 161, 162, 163, 164, 166, 167, 168, 169, 178, 187, 197, 207, 232, 235, 237, 241, 266
pronouns of address, 70, 73, 74, 78, 97, 105, 106, 109, 127, 244
pronunciation, 72, 73, 74, 77, 80, 81, 83, 85, 99, 112, 124. *See also* phonology
proof correction, *see* proofreading, stop-press correction
proof correctors, 206
proofreading, 133, 136, 149, 150, 156, 159, 160, 161, 199, 206, 221. *See also* stop-press correction
proof pages, 149
proof sheets, 206
prose, 68, 75, 77, 116, 117, 119
prosody, *see* meter
proverbs, 77, 82, 90, 94, 124, 125
Public Records, 61, 62
publishers/publishing, 30, 43, 136, 149, 156, 161, 166, 186, 233, 235
punctuation, 34, 68, 70, 71, 73, 77, 78, 79, 107, 112, 144, 198, 199, 200, 201, 202, 203, 204, 205, 207, 218,

INDEX II: SUBJECTS 133

222, 225, 230, 237, 237a, 238
puns, 80, 85, 86, 87, 99, 126, 256. *See also* wordplay
Puritan Widow, see apocryphal and attributed works
Puttenham, George, 103, 114

quartos, 30, 43, 133, 143, 144, 145, 147, 151, 156, 157, 160, 161, 169, 183, 185, 186, 192, 213, 223, 235, 237a
—Bad Quartos, 57, 92, 96, 133, 135, 137, 143, 145, 147, 157, 160, 170, 171, 172, 173, 174, 177, 178, 179, 180, 181, 182, 183, 184, 185, 186, 208, 213, 218, 219, 236
—census of, 139, 140
—comparison with Folio texts, 188, 190, 191, 192, 193, 194, 197, 219, 225
—in concordance, 92
—as copy for First Folio, 133, 156, 161, 167, 168, 169, 170, 207
—discrimination of Bad and Good, 30, 57, 133, 135, 136, 169, 170, 173, 174, 177, 179, 180, 181, 183, 184, 185, 186, 208, 213
—Doubtful Quartos, 136, 213
—economics of publication, 136, 233
—facsimiles, 135, 137, 138
—Good Quartos, 133, 135, 137, 145, 172, 173, 174, 179, 180, 183, 184, 186, 208, 213, 267
—Pavier quartos, 133, 155, 156, 183
—punctuation of, 70, 107, 112, 198, 199, 200, 201
—spelling of, 107. *See also* memorial reconstruction, performance texts, revision, Shakespeare, William (individual works)
Queen Elizabeth, 38, 65, 237a
Quiney, Richard, 42
Quiney, Thomas, 44, 50

Rainolde, Richard, 114
Raleigh, Sir Walter, 65
rare words, 123, 179, 257, 262
"red light" tests, 258
regional language, *see* dialect
registers, 73, 75, 99
relative pronouns, 244, 262
repetitions, 179
reporter, 177, 180, 183, 185
reporting, 161, 170, 172, 176, 179, 181
reviser, 177, 193
revision, 175, 189, 218, 233, 248
—authorial, 157, 160, 169, 182, 187, 188, 190, 191, 192, 193, 194, 195, 196, 197, 213, 226, 228, 237
—nonauthorial, 161, 166, 177, 228
—in *Sir Thomas More*, 263, 264, 266. *See also* abridgment, adaptation, performance texts
rhetoric, 69, 70, 71, 72, 73, 75, 76, 77, 78, 79, 100, 101, 102, 103, 104, 108, 114, 115, 152, 199, 237, 237a, 265
rhetorical figures, 68, 76, 78, 100, 102, 103, 114, 115, 119
rhetorical phrasing, 203
rhyme, 72, 83, 85, 118, 179, 230
Richard of Gloucester (*3 Henry VI*), 108
Riverside Shakespeare, 92, 93
Robertson, J. M., 187
"Roman" style, 75
Rosalind (*As You Like It*), 105
Rose Playhouse, 266
Rowe, Nicholas, 35, 206, 223
Rubinstein, Frankie, 87, 89
running titles, 159
Sadler, Hamnet, 44
Sadler, Judith, 44
sales (of books), 141, 149
Salusbury, Sir John, 51
salutations, 127
scatology, *see* bawdy
Schmidt, Alexander, 93
Schoenbaum, S., 30, 49, 57, 66

Sclater, William, 259, 260
scribes/scriveners, 107, 112, 161, 165, 166, 179, 190
"second best bed," 50, 56, 59, 66
Second Part of the Troublesome Reign of King John, see apocryphal and attributed works
sentence structure, 70, 78, 98, 101, 110, 116, 119, 120, 203
setting by formes, 160
sexual language, *see* bawdy
Shakeshafte, William, 41, 45, 48, 51, 58, 59
Shakespeare, Anne (wife) (Hathaway, Anne), 33, 50, 51, 56, 58, 59
Shakespeare Birthplace Trust, 42
Shakespeare, Hamnet (son), 35
Shakespeare (history of the name), 30
Shakespeare, John (father), 28, 36, 39, 51, 62, 63
Shakespeare, Judith (daughter), 35, 44, 56
Shakespeare, Susanna (Hall, Susanna, daughter), 35, 44, 50, 52, 55, 56
Shakespeare, William (individual works)
—*All's Well*, 47
—*As You Like It*, 47, 75, 105, 130, 239
—*Antony*, 76, 98, 251
—*Comedy of Errors*, 157
—*Contention*, see 2 Henry VI
—*Coriolanus*, 122, 127, 241, 267
—*Hamlet*, 38, 47, 57, 76, 92, 126, 135, 137, 139, 157, 167, 168, 179, 181, 183, 184, 185, 192, 193, 195, 205, 211, 214, 219, 227, 237a, 239
—*1 Henry IV*, 47, 72, 110, 122, 127, 137, 139, 236, 251
—*2 Henry IV*, 72, 110, 127, 137, 139, 157, 167, 168, 195, 214
—*Henry V*, 72, 75, 92, 110, 137, 139, 143, 147, 157, 179, 183, 185, 214, 251
—*1 Henry VI*, 72, 143, 243, 253
—*2 Henry VI*, 51, 57, 72, 92, 135, 137, 139, 143, 179, 180, 182, 184, 241, 243, 251, 253
—*3 Henry VI*, 51, 57, 72, 92, 108, 135, 137, 139, 143, 179, 182, 243, 251, 253
—*Henry VIII*, 72, 104, 243, 244, 262
—*Julius Caesar*, 139, 251
—*King John*, 72, 241
—*King Lear*, 76, 104, 106, 122, 133, 137, 139, 150, 153, 157, 167, 170, 175, 176, 189, 190, 191, 192, 194, 195, 196, 197, 213, 214, 225, 252
—*Lover's Complaint*, 258
—*Love's Labour's Lost*, 51, 137, 139, 143, 192, 195, 239
—*Macbeth*, 75, 76, 126, 139, 157, 193, 236, 244, 250
—*Measure for Measure*, 87, 122, 166
—*Merchant of Venice*, 76, 108, 137, 139, 198, 201
—*Merry Wives*, 38, 74, 92, 110, 137, 139, 143, 147, 157, 171, 177, 178, 179, 181, 183, 185, 193, 219, 239
—*Midsummer Night's Dream*, 51, 137, 139, 157, 195, 239
—*Much Ado*, 104, 106, 122, 137, 139
—*Othello*, 47, 76, 92, 104, 115, 122, 137, 139, 157, 167, 168, 188, 190, 191, 192, 195, 214
—*Pericles*, 57, 92, 135, 137, 139, 147, 157, 181, 183, 220, 243, 244, 247, 248, 250
—*Phoenix and the Turtle*, 51
—*Poems* 1640, 235
—*Rape of Lucrece*, 138, 252
—*Richard II*, 47, 72, 76, 98, 126, 127, 137, 139, 157, 195, 199, 235, 251
—*Richard III*, 51, 72, 76, 115, 133, 137, 139, 157, 167, 170, 213, 241
—*Romeo and Juliet*, 76, 92, 126, 135, 137, 139, 143, 147, 157, 173, 179, 180, 183, 185, 192, 195, 214, 237, 241

INDEX II: SUBJECTS 135

—*Sonnets*, 34, 47, 57, 76, 87, 88, 120, 126, 138, 195, 200, 210
—*Taming of the Shrew*, 139, 143, 219, 236, 239, 243
—*Tempest*, 76, 157, 220, 239
—*Timon of Athens*, 76, 122, 157, 244, 250
—*Titus*, 51, 135, 139, 143, 147, 231, 253
—*Troilus*, 70, 137, 139, 149, 153, 157, 167, 188, 191, 192, 193, 195, 200, 214, 267
—*True Tragedy*, see *3 Henry VI*
—*Two Gentlemen*, 157
—*Two Noble Kinsmen*, 92, 132, 242, 243, 244, 246, 248, 250, 259
—*Venus and Adonis*, 76, 107, 138, 252
—*Winter's Tale*, 75, 115, 126. See also apocryphal and attributed works
Shakespeare, William (life)
—actor, 28, 38, 41, 43, 47
—ancestry, 39, 41, 46
—arrival in London, 28, 30, 57
—birthplace, 53
—businessman, 52
—butcher in boyhood, 28, 57
—Catholicism, 39, 51, 57
—coat of arms, 35
—departure from Stratford-upon-Avon, 33
—education, 38, 39, 46, 51
—humour, 31
—knowledge of Latin and Greek, 28, 32, 57
—knowledge of law, 41, 57, 91
—legends, 28, 30, 33, 34, 35, 37, 38, 39, 49, 57, 59, 64, 210
—"lost years," 51
—marriage licence, 33, 51
—moneylending, 52
—myths, *see* legends
—periods of artistic life, 31
—portraits, 30, 60, 64, 161
—property, purchase and ownership of, 42, 50, 53, 55, 60, 62
—protestantism, 51
—reading, 253
—roles performed, 38, 47
—schoolmaster, 28, 51, 57
—signatures, 40, 50, 56, 60, 62, 267
—spiritual history, 31
—Stratford-upon-Avon, 28, 30, 32, 35, 38, 39, 41, 42, 43, 44, 51, 54, 55, 62
—"Sweet Swan of Avon," 32
—trained as law clerk, 57
—will, 29, 35, 50, 52, 56, 59, 61, 62. See also allusions to Shakespeare, Arden family, Belott-Mountjoy suit, Blackfriars Gate-House, Blackfriars Playhouse, Catholicism, Globe Playhouse, handwriting, Hathaway family, New Place, Welcombe enclosure
Shakespearean Originals, 240
Shakespeare's Birthplace, 53
SHAXICON, 47, 262
Shelley, Percy Bysshe, 252
shorthand, 83, 161, 170, 171, 175, 176, 183
short quartos, *see* Bad Quartos
Sidney, Sir Philip, 120
Sir John Oldcastle, see apocryphal and attributed works
Sir Thomas More, see apocryphal and attributed works
skeleton-formes, 202
socialized editions, 234
sociolinguistics, 69, 104, 106, 244
soliloquy, 75
songs, 118
speech headings, 92, 143, 148, 156, 164, 165, 170, 209, 217, 218, 222, 225, 237a, 241
spelling (and orthography), 68, 70, 71, 73, 74, 77, 78, 80, 83, 107, 112, 124, 144, 161, 209, 215, 218, 222, 224, 230, 237a, 250, 251, 261, 264, 265, 267
stage directions, 92, 151, 156, 161,

163, 164, 170, 213, 217, 222, 225, 231, 237a, 250
Stallybrass, Peter, 216
Stationers' Company, 161
Stationers' Register, 60, 151, 156, 249
Statute against Abuses, 128, 188
stenography, 175
"stolne and surreptitious copies," 145, 147, 179, 183
stop-press correction, 136, 150, 160, 221. *See also* proofreading
Strachey, William, 261
Strange, Lord, 45, 51, 54
stress, 69, 74, 78, 80, 83, 85, 97, 99, 111. *See also* meter
structural parallels, 250
style, 71, 75, 77, 78, 98, 101, 116, 127, 257, 264
stylometrics/stylometry, 250, 257, 259, 260
substantives, 215
"substantive" texts, 213, 222
surveys, 67, 134
suspect texts, *see* Bad Quartos
swearing, *see* oaths
syllabic variants, 120
syntax, 68, 69, 70, 71, 72, 73, 75, 77, 78, 97, 98, 101, 110, 111, 117, 119, 261
Syrus, Publilius, *Sententiae*, 90

Taming of a Shrew, *see* apocryphal and attributed works
Tanselle, G. Thomas, 232
taxonomy, 68
Taylor, Gary, 190, 194, 196, 216
textual bibliography, 131, 132
textual criticism and theory, 131, 132, 134, 153, 163, 185, 186, 189, 206, 212, 216, 218, 219, 237, 237a
textual problems, *see* textual criticism and theory
textual variation, 188, 191, 193, 194, 195, 196, 197, 226, 227, 230, 237

theatrical managers, 161
theatrical manuscripts, 213. *See also* part, plot, promptbooks
theatrical provenance, 250
themes, 248, 253
thematic parallels, 264, 265, 267
Theobald, Lewis, 35, 223; *Double Falsehood*, 248
Thomas Lord Cromwell, *see* apocryphal and attributed works
Thomson, Peter, 66
"thou/you," *see* pronouns of address
through line numbering, 136, 222
Tilley, Morris Palmer, 82, 90, 94, 125
Tilney, Edmund, 263
titles (of books), 225
title pages, 29, 151, 155, 183, 249
Top, Alexander, *Oliue Leafe*, 203
touring companies, 171, 178, 236
Tragedy of Richard III, *see* apocryphal and attributed works
transcripts, 144, 150, 151, 154, 161, 166, 167, 169
transmission of texts, 131, 223, 233
Troublesome Reign of King John, *see* apocryphal and attributed works
Tudor educational curriculum, 102
two hours, 158
types, 131, 133, 150, 155, 159, 161, 183, 224, 225

unauthorized publication, 183. *See also* piracy
uncertainty, 216, 229, 234, 237, 256
unediting, 212, 225, 237a
Ur-*Hamlet*, *see* apocryphal and attributed works
Urkowitz, Steven, 190, 194

variants, *see* press variants
variety, linguistic, 72, 74
verbal parallels, 250, 252, 253, 254, 256, 257, 258, 261, 262, 263, 264, 265

INDEX II: SUBJECTS

verse forms, 68, 179
"Verses on John Combe," *see* apocryphal and attributed works
verse tests, 249
versification (Shakespeare's), 77, 248, 261
vocabulary, 68, 69, 70, 72, 73, 74, 75, 77, 78, 79, 93, 96, 98, 109, 123, 130, 152, 179, 248, 250, 251, 254, 255, 256, 257, 261, 262, 264, 265. *See also* bawdy, dictionaries

warfare, language of, 84
Warren, Michael, 190, 194, 196, 216
Warwickshire, 38, 41, 73, 124
watermarks, 155, 183
Webster, John, 117, 264, 265
Welcombe enclosure, 42, 60
Wells, Stanley, 57, 216, 229, 260
Whateley, Anne [Annam], 33, 65. *See also* Shakspeare, Anne

Wheeler, Margaret, 44
Wilkins, George, 244
Williams, Gordon, 89
Willis, John, 175
Willobie His Avisa, *see* apocryphal and attributed works
Wilson, John Dover, 178, 187, 232
Wilson, Thomas, 114
Woodstock, *see* apocryphal and attributed works
Worcester County Record Office, 53
word-formation, 70, 73, 75, 100, 109, 111, 113, 123. *See also* innovation, neologisms, vocabulary
wordplay, 68, 70, 77, 116, 126, 130, 256. *See also* puns
Wright, William Aldis, 207
W. S., 245, 250, 259, 260, 261

Yorkshire Tragedy, *see* apocryphal and attributed works

MICHAEL WARREN, editor of this eighth volume, is Professor Emeritus of English Literature at University of California, Santa Cruz. He has published *The Division of the Kingdoms: Shakespeare's Two Versions of 'King Lear'* (co-edited with Gary Taylor), *The Complete 'King Lear' 1608–1623*, and *The Parallel 'King Lear' 1608–1623*, and numerous articles on the texts of English drama.

SHAKESPEARE: LIFE, LANGUAGE AND LINGUISTICS, TEXTUAL STUDIES, AND THE CANON is a guide to published resources concerning four important and fundamental areas of Shakespeare research.

Life: The major sources of information and of reproductions of documents; citations for the significant narratives and interpretations of the biographical evidence published during the last three centuries.

Language and linguistics: Books and articles about the distinctive historical features of Shakespeare's language; discussions of grammar and rhetoric, verse and prose, and vocabulary and imagery; dictionaries, concordances, and guides to pronunciation.

Textual studies (the longest section, since this is a challenging field): Facsimiles of the earliest texts and major studies in the long history of Shakespearean bibliography, particularly the twentieth-century's debates concerning Good and Bad Quartos, revision, and (emphasized) editorial theory and practice.

Canon: Information on works that either constitute or examine the constitution of the Shakespeare canon; studies of four works whose current relation to the canon are the subject of significant scholarly debate illustrate the issues of authorship and attribution.

Selective, clearly and fully annotated, this bibliography provides scholars, students, and general readers the means to explore with confidence four major areas in Shakespeare studies.

PEGASUS SHAKESPEARE BIBLIOGRAPHIE(S)

The Pegasus Shakespeare Bibliographies — to total 12 volumes — pro(vide) handy and authoritative guides to Shakespeare scholarship and critic(ism). They are prepared for faculty and students in universities and college(s as) well as in high schools. Edited by leading scholar/teachers of Shakespe(are,) each volume is organized for ease of use. There are approximately (200?) entries per volume of 160 pages; these have been selected as the best (and) most useful books and essays. The editors include only work of (high) quality or significant influence; partisanship is carefully avoided.

Most importantly, the annotations are full and helpful. The edi(tors) describe each item clearly so that a reader can quickly tell wheth(er a) particular essay or book would be useful. Cross-references and rich (in)dexes complement the convenient organization of entries. So, with m(ini)mal effort, a reader will be able to find the right critical or schol(arly) resources. Additionally, the full annotations provide a good grasp (of) Shakespeare criticism and scholarship.

**THE BOOKS ARE EMINENTLY USER-FRIENDLY,
AND THE LOW PRICE ($9.95 PER VOLUME) IS FANTASTIC!**

Each volume includes most or all of the following sections:
- Editions and Reference Works
- Authorship, Dating, Textual Studies
- Influences; Sources; Historical and Intellectual Backgrounds
- Language and Linguistics
- Criticism
- Stage History and Performance Criticism
- Reception History
- Adaptations
- Teaching and Collections of Essays
- Bibliographies
- Author & Subject Indexes

Send orders to our distributor—
Cornell University Press Services
750 Cascadilla Street
PO Box 6525
Ithaca, New York 14851
Email: orderbook@cupserv.org

PEGASUS SHAKESPEARE BIBLIOGRAPHIES

Volumes in Print

Love's Labor's Lost, A Midsummer Night's Dream, and The Merchant of Venice. Ed. Clifford Chalmers Huffman (1995) 0-86698-177-2

King Lear and Macbeth. Ed. Rebecca W. Bushnell (1996) 1-889818-00-3

Shakespeare and the Renaissance Stage to 1616 / Shakespearean Stage History 1616 to 1998. Ed. Hugh Macrae Richmond (1999) 1-889818-22-4

Richard II, 1 and 2 Henry IV, and Henry V. Ed. Joseph Candido (1998) 1-889818-10-0

Hamlet. Ed. Michael E. Mooney (1999) 1-889818-21-6

The Rape of Lucrece, Titus Andronicus, Julius Caesar, Antony and Cleopatra, and Coriolanus. Ed. Clifford Chalmers Huffman and John W. Velz (2002) 1-889818-30-5

Cymbeline, The Winter's Tale, and The Tempest. Ed. John S. Mebane (2002) 1-889818-31-3

Shakespeare: Life, Language & Linguistics, Textual Studies, and The Canon. Ed. Michael Warren (2002) 1-889818-34-8

As You Like It, Much Ado About Nothing, and Twelfth Night, or What You Will. Ed. Marilyn L. Williamson (2003) 1-889818-35-6

Volumes in Preparation

Jean Howard on Shakespeare criticism and literary theory

Jill Levenson on *Romeo and Juliet* and *Othello*

Barbara Traister on *Troilus and Cressida, Measure for Measure,* and *All's Well That Ends Well*

Price for each volume: $9.95.
Discounts for standing orders.